Excel Formulas: Halfwit to Hero

Matthew MacDonald

Excel Formulas: Halfwit to Hero

Published by ProseTech

Toronto, Ontario

2018:   First Edition

Online resources for this book are available at

http://lab.halfwit2hero.com/excelformulas

A book from the Halfwit to Hero series

http://halfwif2hero.com

For information about translations, academic use, and bulk purchases, email matthew@prosetech.com

ISBN-13: 978-1-7753737-0-4

About the Author

Matthew MacDonald has helped thousands of people learn to write code, build websites, and tame giant spreadsheets. He's a three-time Microsoft MVP and the author of more than two dozen books for publishers including O'Reilly, McGraw-Hill, Apress, Microsoft Press, Wrox, and No Starch Press. He's also taught the mystical ways of programming at Ryerson University and Sheridan College.

Matthew's Excel roots go deep—he published his first book about the wonderful world of Excel spreadsheets in 2005 and wrote the best-selling *Excel 2013: The Missing Manual*. Those who don't have tech problems to solve can check out Matthew's science books, where he explores the quirks and complexities of the human brain (*Your Brain: The Missing Manual*) and body (*Your Body: The Missing Manual*). Both books use a mash-up of full-color pictures, trivia, and philosophical head-scratchers.

Matthew lives in Toronto with his wife and three daughters. You can contact him at matthew@prosetech.com.

Contents

Welcome Aboard...

"A journey of a thousand miles begins with a single click."

Welcome to *Excel Formulas: Halfwit to Hero*, a compact, no-fluff introduction to formula writing in Excel. It's written by Matthew MacDonald (that's me), author of the bestselling *Excel 2013: The Missing Manual* (O'Reilly, 2013) and dozens of other books about computers and technology. But as you're about to see, this book is a bit different.

About the "Halfwit to Hero" Series

Over the past decade and a half, I've written dozens of massive books for nearly every tech publisher in existence. Many of them can be found in classrooms and offices around the world, often holding down stacks of paper or propping open heavy doors.

Writing big books is a lot of work, which is fine (after all, it's my problem). But *reading* big books can also be a lot of work, and that, unfortunately, becomes *your* problem. After all, wading through an ocean of text isn't the easiest way to pick up a new skill. And what good is all the knowledge in the world if you need a week off to find the stuff you really need?

That's why I decided to launch the Halfwit to Hero series to focus on tutorial-based learning. Unlike the hefty doorstops of the past, Halfwit to Hero books have tightly focused chapters and a strict no-dozing-allowed policy. Most importantly, each Halfwit to Hero book has a tutorial website that gets you to practice every new concept. In other words, the Halfwit to Hero series forces you to apply what you learn before it drops out of your brain.

Yes, this approach requires more work than breezing through the book on your sofa while watching The Bachelor in the background. But the payoff is immense. Instead of ending this book as a person who's "kind of" familiar with Excel, you'll be someone who's developed real Excel skills. And when someone asks you about an Excel formula feature, your reaction won't be "That sounds vaguely familiar"—it will be "I tried that out myself."

The Twelve-Year-Old Test

Ever struggled to learn from a book, only to be derailed by an obvious mistake or something that didn't work the way it was supposed to? To prevent these types of problems, every Halfwit to Hero book is double-checked by a genuine beginner.

Excel Formulas: Halfwit to Hero, has successfully passed the hardest beginner challenge: the *twelve-year-old test*. That means a motivated twelve-year-old successfully completely all of its tutorials, with only a minimum of adult help.

Who Should Read This Book

This book is for anyone who wants to learn to write formulas in Excel. This book doesn't teach you how to use Excel's other features (for example, charts). However, formulas are the heart and soul of Excel. They're an excellent place to start your Excel journey, whether you're using Excel to build a business, run a budget, or solve your math homework. The end of this book has some suggestions for next steps, once you've become a formula hero.

If you've never cracked open an Excel spreadsheet, don't panic! Chapter 1 of this book, "What You Should Already Know," explains four essential Excel concepts. If you're a beginner, you can quickly review these basics before you get started writing formulas.

What You Need to Use This Book

Not much! You can use almost any version of Excel. Just pick from this list:

▶ **Excel 2016** is the traditional desktop version of Excel that runs on Windows computers and has all the bells and whistles.

▶ **Excel 2013 and Excel 2010** are older versions of Excel. They have the same formula system, ribbon, and menu commands as Excel 2016 (more or less). That means you can use this book without any headaches.

▶ **Excel 2019** hasn't been released yet. But you'll be relieved to know that it handles formula writing in the same way as earlier Excel versions.

▶ **Excel Online** is a slimmed-down version of Excel that runs in your web browser. Excel Online has fewer features than its big brother, but most of the formula concepts in this book still apply. Best of all, it's 100% free. The most important difference is that Excel Online makes you store all your spreadsheets online in your Microsoft OneDrive account. To try it out, visit https://office.live.com/start/Excel.aspx

▶ **Excel 2016 for Mac** is the Apple-friendly version of Excel, and it's probably the most different option in this list. If you have Excel for Mac, you can still use this book to learn the art of formula writing. But expect some differences when this book talks about the buttons in the ribbon (the super toolbar at the top of the Excel window), because the layout isn't the same.

Pro tip: If you have an Office 365 subscription, you're in good shape for this book. You'll get the latest version of Excel on your computer, automatically. A year of Office 365 is often included when you buy a new computer.

The Tutorial Website

To get your money's worth from this book, you need to practice your skills. Don't wait until the end of the last chapter. It's much better if you practice each new concept before your brain tosses it in the mental trash bin.

There are two types of practice sections in this book.

▶ The "Try it out" sections invite you to experiment with something new right away. All you need is to have your computer close by.

▶ The numbered exercise sections, like "Exercise #1: Calculate averages," are more interesting. They correspond to exercises on the tutorial web site, at http://lab.halfwit2hero.com/excelformulas. Most exercises give you a starter spreadsheet and lead you through a sequence of steps that you must perform with that spreadsheet. Along the way, you'll be asked to figure out some details on your own. If you're not sure, there's always a CLICK TO REVEAL button hiding the answer, as well as a solution spreadsheet that shows the finished result.

If you're curious about these exercises, you can check out the tutorial website right now. If not, turn the page and *let's begin*.

What You Should Already Know

"Beware the unknown unknowns—the things you don't know that you don't know."

This book is about the art of writing Excel formulas. If you're already comfortable starting Excel, opening a spreadsheet, and poking around, you're ready to move on. Jump straight to Chapter 2 to start crunching numbers.

But if you're new to Excel, don't despair! This chapter will fill you in on the *four most essential* Excel concepts. You'll learn how to zip around the Excel window, put numbers and text into a simple spreadsheet, and save your work. And once you practice the super-short exercises in this chapter, you'll be an Excel newbie no more.

Step 0: Starting Excel for the First Time

This one isn't actually a concept. Before you can do anything in Excel, you need to start it and create a blank new *workbook* (that's the official word for the Excel spreadsheet file that stores your work).

In older versions of Excel (like Excel 2010), you simply find the green Excel icon, click it, and you're off. Excel drops you into the worksheet grid, ready to work.

Newer versions of Excel, like Excel 2016, try to be more helpful by presenting a *welcome page* first. On the left of the welcome page is a list of spreadsheets that you've worked on recently. On the right of the welcome page is a gallery of ready-made starter spreadsheets.

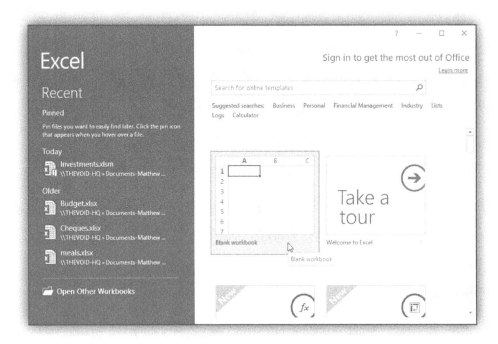

The best way to keep things simple is to start with a completely blank spreadsheet. Click the "Blank workbook" picture to create one.

That's it!

What about Excel Online?

Excel Online is a version of Excel that runs in your web browser. Even though it's free, it manages to offer the most important features from "ordinary" Excel. So if you don't actually have a full version of Excel on your computer, you can still do almost everything in Excel Online.

The main difference between ordinary Excel and Excel Online is that the ordinary version lets you save workbook files on your computer. If you're using Excel Online, you need to store all your Excel files online in your Microsoft OneDrive account (that's also free). And if you lose your Internet connection for whatever reason, you'll be forced to stop working.

To launch Excel Online, type this address into your favorite web browser:

https://office.live.com/start/Excel.aspx

Or just search for "Excel Online" in Google.

When you start Excel Online, you'll see a welcome page that looks almost the same as in ordinary Excel, with a list of recent files and some starter spreadsheets. Click "Blank workbook" to begin with a blank canvas.

Explaining the Excel jargon

Here are some words that you should get clear on right now:

▶ A *workbook* is an Excel file. It stores your spreadsheet (either on your computer, or in on online account.)

▶ A workbook can hold one or more work*sheets*. The worksheet is the grid with all the cells in it. Right now, you're only interested in workbooks that have one worksheet. You can get fancier later.

▶ A *spreadsheet* is the same thing as a workbook. But other programs that aren't Excel, like Google Sheets, use the word spreadsheet instead of the word workbook.

1. Your Best Friend the Ribbon

At the top of the Excel window is a super toolbar called the *ribbon*. If you can't find the Excel feature you want in here, odds are it doesn't exist.

The ribbon is organized into tabs. Click a different tab, and you'll see a different set of buttons. The idea is to group features together logically, so it's easier to find what you want.

The ribbon is packed full of Excel features. If you need to get something done with Excel, you'll find it in here. For example, you can set calculation options in the **Formulas** tab and set printer margins in the **Page Layout** tab. Sometimes, new tabs will appear to help you with special tasks (like formatting a chart or tweaking a picture).

If you haven't tried it already, now's a good time to click through the tabs in the ribbon. You'll notice that the **File** tab doesn't behave like the others. If you click it, Excel shows a new page where with options for opening, saving, and printing files. (More on that at the end of this chapter.)

In this book, most of your work takes place in the worksheet grid, but every once in a while you'll need to use a command in the ribbon. To point you to the right spot, we tell you the tab to click, the section of the tab to look in, and the button to click. For example, to change the margins for your worksheet printout, you need to click **Page Layout ▷ Page Setup ▷ Margins**. (In other words, go to the **Page Layout** tab, look in the **Page Setup** section, and click the **Margins** button.)

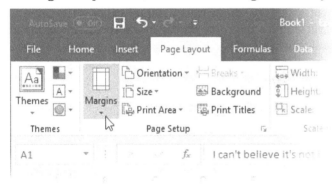

If the ribbon is hogging up too much space, you can temporarily clear it out of the way. To do that, double-click one of the tab titles (any one except **File**), or press the shortcut key combination **Ctrl+F1**. Excel will shrink the ribbon down so that all you can see is the tab titles. Double-click the tab or press **Ctrl+F1** again to restore the ribbon.

To use a command when the ribbon is collapsed, click a tab, and the ribbon will pop into view temporarily. When you click back on your worksheet, the ribbon will shrink away once more.

2. The Worksheet Grid

Every Excel workbook is divided into a grid of boxes, called *cells*. You can type in any of these cells. You'll use them to write your headings, captions, dates, numbers, and calculations. At first, all these cells are blank.

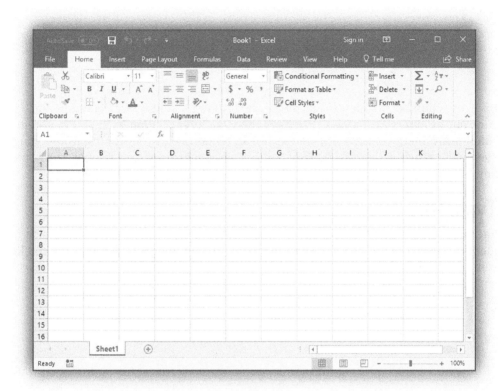

One cell has a dark black outline around it. (Right now, it's the one in the top-left corner.) This is where you're currently positioned in your worksheet. If you start typing (anything—try some random gibberish!) it appears in this cell. Press **Enter** when you're finished.

Moving around the grid

To move to another cell, use the arrow keys. Or to move faster, hit the **Page Down** and **Page Up** keys. (And of course you can click your way around with the mouse too.)

Excel worksheets are *big*. If you get carried away, you can scroll down to the very bottom, which is row 1,048,576. The row number shows up in the margin on the left.

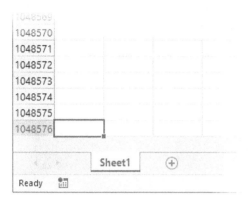

Excel uses numbers to identify each row and letters to identify each column. When it runs out of letters, it doubles or triples them, so after column X, Y, and Z, you get column AA, then AB, then AC, and so on. Scroll all the way to the right any you'll eventually reach column XFD. This is the Excel wilderness, and people rarely put anything way out here.

Typing in a cell

Each cell is a separate "slot" that can hold information. Later on, you'll get use to identifying each cell using its column letter and row number. For example, the cell **E6** is in column E, row 6.

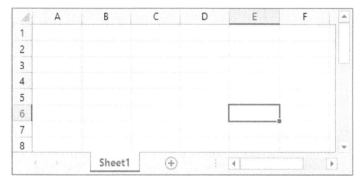

It's easy to start filling in the cells of your worksheet. For example, if you type the word "horses" in first column of the first row, then you press the down key and type "bananas", then you press the right arrow key and type "64", you'll have filled three cells with information.

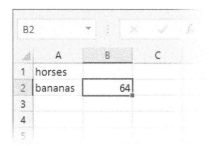

If you move onto a cell that already has something in it and you start typing, your new entry replaces your old one. In other words, if you move to cell B2 in the previous example (the one that has "bananas" in it) and you type "apple" you'll end up replacing one fruit for another.

Pro tip: As in most Windows programs, you can undo a bad edit right after you make it by pressing **Ctrl+Z**.

Exercise #1: Find the cell

If you feel like a complete Excel newcomer, and you're not comfortable referring to cells with names like A1 or E6, here's an exercise to try.

Head to http://lab.halfwit2hero.com/excelformulas and open the "Find your cell" workbook. It leads you on an Excel hunt that jumps around the worksheet grid, from one cell to another. By the time you reach the end, you'll be used to Excel's column letters and row numbers.

Overlapping cells

Here's a problem that happens to pretty much everybody in the first fifteen minutes of using Excel: the text in one cell overlaps with the text in another cell.

For example, if you type "I can't believe it's not butter" at the top of the first column (cell A1), and you type "horses" at the top of the second column (that's cell B1), you won't see the whole sentence in cell A1 anymore.

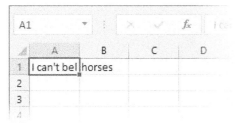

When one cell overlaps another, it's always the stuff that's in the cell on the right that ends up covering some of the stuff that's in the cell on the left.

Chapter 1: What You Should Already Know

Overlapping only happens with text (for example, long headings or sentences). Excel won't let a number leak onto another cell, because than can cause serious confusion.

Overlapping isn't a problem if you're covering a blank cell. In that case, Excel lets your extra long value cover up the empty space. For example, it's common to put a long title in cell A1, and all your headings and numbers in the rows underneath.

But if you're overlapping cell is hiding something, it's not so great. For example, if one column heading is leaking onto another column heading, you'll want to fix that.

Banana Consumption in the United States

Year	Bananas E Cost Per Banana
2018	92 $ 0.24
2017	90 $ 0.22
2016	83 $ 0.23
2015	74 $ 0.29
2014	76 $ 0.28
2013	72 $ 0.15
2012	62 $ 0.15

This long title is not a problem

This long heading is a problem

To fix overlapping cells, you can resize the too-small column that can't fit its contents.

Try it out: Resizing columns

It's easy to fix overlapping cells by widening your problem column. For example, in the "I can't believe it's not better" example shown above, you would widen the A column.

Here's how to widen a column:

1. Look at the column header. That's the gray box at the top of the column that has the column letter in it (like A).

2. Hover your mouse pointer over the *right edge* of the column header until it turns into a funny looking double-arrow icon.

3. Now click and drag the column border to the right. Release the mouse button when the column is the size you want.

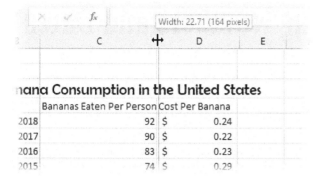

Now that you know how, give this column-resizing technique a try!

There's also a shortcut for nimble clickers. If you double-click the right edge of a column header, Excel automatically resizes the column so it's just large enough to fit the longest value inside, with no overlapping.

Another approach: Wrapping text

Excel gives you another way to fit long bits of text in narrow cells. You can use *text wrapping*, which makes your text flow over several lines, and expands the height of the cell to accommodate it.

To use text wrapping, go to your too-small cell, and click the **Wrap Text** button, which sits in the **Home** ▷ **Alignment** section of the ribbon.

The **Wrap Text** button is easy to overlook, so you may need to move your mouse around until you find the right button. It shows the letters "abc" split over two lines.

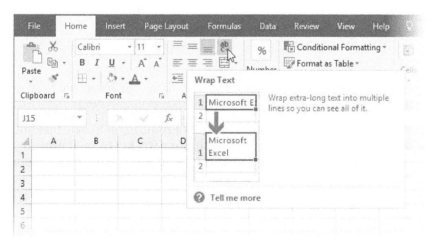

---

3. Understanding Numbers and Dates

It's easy to start filling in your cells. But not all cell values are treated the same.

Excel distinguishes between text, numbers, and dates. It has to, because it needs to be able to *use* the numbers and dates in formulas. In other words, if you type "horseshoe" in a cell, Excel realizes that it's just a piece of text. But if you type "72", Excel realizes it has something much more useful: a number.

Interestingly, Excel has a little tipoff that reveals its thinking. When you type a number into a cell and press **Enter**, Excel automatically lines the number up with the right side of the cell. But when you type in text, Excel doesn't change the alignment.

```
This is text
more text here
                23405
                  520
                19302
```

Excel uses right-alignment because that usually makes long columns of numbers easier to read and compare. Of course, you can change the alignment of any cell using the formatting commands in the **Home** ▷ **Alignment** section of the ribbon. But the important fact to understand right now is that Excel notices your numbers.

Pro tip: Never put text and numbers into the same cell. For example, if you type "72 horseshoes" in one cell, Excel treats that as one piece of text and ignores the number part. That means you can't perform calculations with it. For the same reason, you shouldn't type more than one number in the same cell (as in "72, 26").

Dates

Excel isn't only interested in numbers. It also recognizes dates. However, you need to be careful to enter your dates in one of the formats that Excel understands.

For example, if you type "January 15, 2019" and press **Enter**, Excel knows that you typed in a date. But if you have a pile of dates to put into a worksheet, you probably don't want to write out the full name of each month. Instead, you can use one of these shorter date formats:

▶ 15-Jan-19

▶ 2019-1-15

▶ 1/15/2019

The last format only works if your computer is set up with U.S. region settings. In some other countries, the order of days and months is switched around.

There's a good reason to get Excel to recognize your dates. If Excel knows a cell has a date, it's able to use that date for sorting lists and performing calculations. For example, if you're wondering how many days are between now and your 87th birthday, Excel can calculate that in a breeze. You'll learn how in Chapter 5.

Formatting numbers and dates

What's the difference between 42200, $42200, 4,220.00, and 4.22E+04? From Excel's point of view, nothing much. It's just four different ways of displaying the same number.

This approach makes a lot of sense. It means you don't need to worry about trying to make your numbers look nice when you type them in. Instead, you can fill your cells with ordinary numbers, and then use Excel's formatting features to change what they look like.

It's all very quick and painless. Just move to the cell that has the number you want to format. Then, look in the **Home** ▷ **Number** section of the ribbon. You'll see a box that shows the current number format. (Usually, that's the boring General format.) To try something else, click the drop-down arrow to show the list.

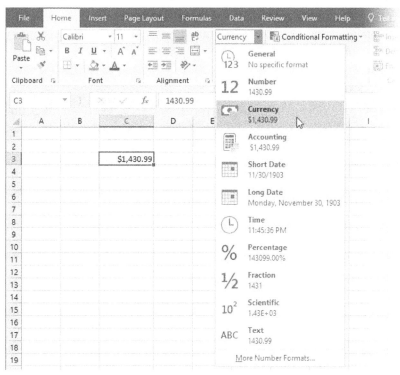

For example, picking the Currency format gets you a currency symbol (that's the dollar sign), a thousands-separator comma, and two decimal places to show the number of cents. The Accounting format is similar, except it adds some space between the currency symbol and the number, and it puts brackets around negative values.

Don't be afraid to try out different number formats. You can easily change back. You can also explore the other buttons in the **Home** ▷ **Number** section of the ribbon. They let you change the currency symbol, show commas, and add or hide decimal places.

And just as you can format numbers, you can do the same with dates. For example, a click in the number format list can take you from a short date format like 3/30/2018 to a long date format like "Friday, March 30, 2018."

Remember, when you format a number or date, you don't change the actual value. You just change what it looks like on the worksheet. (If you're not sure you believe this, there's a simple test you can try. Click the cell that has the number and then look in the formula bar, just above the worksheet grid. There you'll see the plain number or date, with no formatting.)

Exercise #2: Make this look like that

To help all this sink in, you need to format some numbers and dates of your own.

On the tutorial site (http://lab.halfwit2hero.com/excelformulas) there's a workbook named "Make this look like that" that can help you get some practice. It presents a bunch of plain ol' boring numbers and asks you to style each one to match the formatted number in another cell.

Formatting a bunch of cells at once

Sometimes, you'll have a whole pile of numbers that need to be formatted. For example, imagine you fill a worksheet with a list of items you want to sell at your garage sale, and the price of each item. Ordinary numbers work fine, but they don't line up right and they don't have the dollar sign, so they won't *look* like prices.

You already know how to change the format of a cell. But did you know that you can change the format of all these cells at once?

The trick is to *select* all the cells you want to change. One of the easiest ways to select a bunch of cells is to click the letter at the top of a column. For example, if you click the D column heading, Excel selects all the cells underneath. You'll know that they're selected because Excel temporarily shades the cells grey.

Here's an example with the D column selected:

C	D ↓	E
	Prices	
	12.99	
	19.99	
	4.75	
	3.99	
	23.5	
	15.99	

Don't worry if you also end up selecting blank cells and cells with text in them, like column headings. Number formatting only affects numbers and dates.

When you pick a new format from the **Home** ▷ **Number** section of the ribbon, Excel changes the appearance of *all* your selected cells. So if you select the Accounting format, you get this:

C	D	E
	Prices	
	$ 12.99	
	$ 19.99	
	$ 4.75	
	$ 3.99	
	$ 23.50	
	$ 15.99	

Here are two more ways to select a group of cells:

▶ **Using the mouse.** Click the first cell you want to select and, while holding the mouse button down, drag over the other cells you want to select.

▶ **Using the keyboard.** Move to the first cell you want to select. Hold down the **Shift** key, and then use the arrow keys to move up, down, or to the side, selecting as you go.

Now head to the **Home** ▷ **Number** section of the ribbon to format your cells. When you're finished, just click somewhere else on the worksheet to clear your selection and get back to work.

What does ##### mean?

Earlier, you learned that when a piece of text is too big for its cell, you get overlapping. But when a *number* is too wide, Excel decides not to display it at all. Instead, Excel fills the cell with a bunch of useless # symbols.

Small number: 12345678
Big number: ########

This problem doesn't happen too often. That's because Excel usually widens your cells to fit their numbers *automatically*. For example, if you type a really long number into a cell and press **Enter**, Excel resizes the column to accommodate it.

However, Excel doesn't perform its column-resizing magic when you change the number format. So if you switch to a format that has way more decimal places and the number doesn't fit in its cell anymore, you get the ####s. The # symbols also show up if you deliberately shrink a column to be too small for its contents.

Excel's behavior may seem weird, but there's a good reason behind it. If Excel allowed the number in one cell to leak onto a number in another cell, it could look like a completely different number—and that's a surefire way to make a nasty mistake. (For example, imagine if a $1,299 dining table leaks onto a cell that shows the $61.70 in tax, and you end up paying $129961.70 for your furniture.) So instead of allowing a disastrous misunderstanding, Excel does its best to point out the problem and get your attention with ####s.

Now that you know what causes the # symbols to appear, you can fix the problem with a bit of column resizing. As soon as you stretch the column wide enough, the missing number will pop back into view.

4. Saving Your Work

Once you've finished your Excel masterpiece (or if you're just done working for the day), you need to save it in a file.

This isn't difficult, but it may be slightly different depending on your version of Excel. In most versions of Excel, you start by clicking the **File** tab, which is the first tab in the ribbon. That pulls up a new list of commands (on the left) that deal with tasks like saving, opening, and printing your work.

To save your workbook, click **Save As** in the list of commands. Excel shows some folders that you've recently used when saving or opening workbooks. (In the example above, these are Sample, Desktop, and Financial).

If you see the folder you want to use, click it, type in a name for your workbook, and click the **Save** button to seal the deal.

If you don't see the folder you want to use, click **Browse** to hunt around on your hard drive for the right place.

Here's one more option: If you have a free Microsoft OneDrive account, you can store your work online. To do that, click OneDrive, then click the Sign In button and supply your OneDrive user name and password. Once you've signed in you'll be able to pick any one of your online folders as the storage location.

Opening a workbook

The File tab also holds the secret to opening a workbook file from inside Excel. Just click the **File** tab, then choose **Open** in the list of commands. Excel will show a list of all the workbooks you've worked on recently.

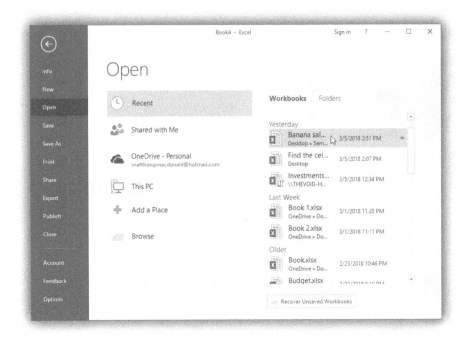

Click the workbook you want to open, or click **Browse** to hunt through your computer's folders in search of some other workbook.

Saving files in Excel Online

Excel Online is a bit different when it comes to saving files. Spoiler alert: when running Excel Online, you never need to save anything. That's because Excel Online *automatically* saves your workbook every time you make a change, from the moment you first create it.

There are a few technical reasons that Excel does this. For one thing, it's possible for several people to edit the same workbook in Excel Online at once, using different computers. This system only works if everyone's changes are saved right away.

Also, online connections can be finicky. It's not worth losing an hour of work because your computer dropped its Wi-Fi signal.

However, even though Excel Online doesn't need you to save anything, you should still use the **File ▷ Save As** command at least once to choose a proper name for your workbook. Until you do, Excel will carry on saving your workbook with a lame autogenerated name like "Book 3.xlsx"

To pick a better name, click the **File** tab, then click **Save As** in the command list, and then click the **Rename** button. Excel will ask you to type in a new, more meaningful file name.

The Last Word

Congratulations! You've just finished a very condensed introduction to the Excel main window. Right now, you should be comfortable starting Excel, creating a workbook, and moving around the worksheet grid. You should also know how to put some text, a number, or a date into any cell. But you don't need to know how to do anything truly useful yet, and that's OK!

In the next chapter, you'll get to the real meat of the matter by writing your first formula.

## Chapter 2

Building Basic Formulas

"To get an answer, you must first ask a question."

Writing an Excel formula is shockingly easy. The trick is to translate the question you have into the language that Excel understands. For example, if you're wondering "How much tax will I pay for a new coffee table?" you need to tell Excel something like this: `=B3*0.04` (Weird, right?)

In this chapter, you'll learn to speak Excel's formula language. You'll start by asking Excel to add, subtract, and divide simple numbers. Along the way, you'll take a short detour back to grade school to revisit the rules for *order of operations* and check out the right way to use brackets.

Starting a Formula

Every Excel formula starts in exactly the same way. You move to a blank cell and announce your intentions by typing the equal sign (=).

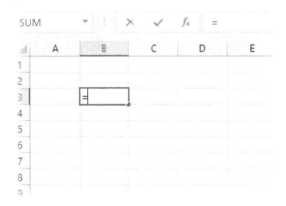

Take a moment to find the equal sign on your keyboard, if you haven't spotted it already. On most keyboards, you'll find the equal sign on the number row, just to the right of all the numbers.

Once you type the equal sign, Excel knows that you are about to type in a formula. A formula can be as simple and short as you want, or it can be a complex beast of a calculation.

The simplest possible formula isn't really a formula at all, but just an equal sign and a single number like this:

=42

In Excel language, this formula says "equals forty-two." The answer to this formula is, unsurprisingly, the number 42.

A slightly more sophisticated formula combines two numbers in addition, subtraction, multiplication, or division. Here's an example:

=1+1

To see a formula in action, find a blank cell in your worksheet, type it in, and then press the **Enter** key to finish up. On your worksheet, you'll see the *solution* to your formula. So if you asked Excel to add =1+8 the number 9 will show up on your worksheet.

TYPE THIS:	SEE THIS:
=1+8	9

Remember, every formula must start with the equal sign. This is right:

=12+36

But this is wrong:

12+36

If you forget the equal sign, Excel assumes you're typing in some text, and doesn't perform any calculations. Instead of seeing the formula result on your worksheet, you'll see exactly what you typed (in this case, that's the text "12+36" instead of the answer, 48).

Can I use the equal sign without starting a formula?

It's not very often that you'll want to start a cell with an equal sign but *not* write a formula. But if the need arises, you'll be glad to know that Excel has you covered. The trick is to type an apostrophe (') before you type the equal sign. The apostrophe tells Excel to treat the cell as ordinary text, no matter what it contains. So if you type '=1+1 rather than just =1+1 Excel assumes that you don't really want a formula. Instead of performing a calculation, Excel shows exactly what you typed (not including the apostrophe).

Editing a Formula

On your worksheet, Excel shows the result of your formula. So if you type a formula that adds two numbers, you'll see the total on your worksheet. However, your original formula still exists—it's just tucked away in the background.

To see your formula, make sure you're in the right cell. (You can move there using the keyboard, or just by clicking the cell with the mouse.). You'll see your original formula in the *formula bar*, which is the editing box that sits at the top of your worksheet, just under the ribbon.

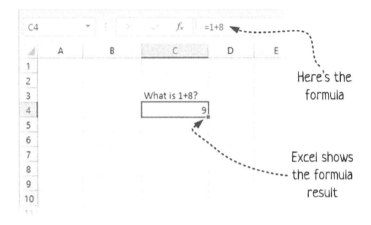

To change your formula, click anywhere in the formula bar. Make your changes, and then press **Enter** to complete them. Once you do, Excel recalculates the formula and shows the new answer in the worksheet.

If you start making a formula change and then decide not to go through with it, press the **Esc** key to cancel your changes.

Pro tip: Keyboard lovers don't need to click in the formula bar to start editing. You can just press the **F2** key to start editing the cell that you're currently on.

Formula Practice

Before you try any fancy formula work, you need to get comfortable with building basic formulas. The best way to do that is to exercise your math skills with the *arithmetic operators*. Those are the symbols that tell Excel to add, subtract, multiply, and divide numbers. Here's your basic toolkit:

▶ Use + to add (so =2+2 is 4)

▶ Use - to subtract (so =6-2 is 4)

▶ Use * to multiply (so =5*6 is 30)

▶ Use / to divide (so =8/2 is 4)

▶ Use ^ to add an exponent (so =3^2 means 3 squared, which is 9)

▶ Use . for decimal values (so =2.5+2.5 is 5)

Let's get one more thing out of the way: spaces are yours to use at your pleasure. So if you want to replace this:

```
=10+8+2
```

with this:

```
=10  +  8  +  2
```

It's all good. Excel doesn't care, and it'll keep your spaces just the way you typed them in. You won't care either, unless you find that adding the spaces makes a complicated formula slightly easier to read. (If so, go crazy with them.)

Try it out: Excel arithmetic

Before you go any further, it's worth firing up your own copy of Excel so you can enter a few simple formulas of your own. Here's how to practice:

1. Move down a column of cells, one at a time. In each cell, type a new, simple formula, like the ones that are shown in the previous list. Press **Enter** each time you finish a formula, and watch the answer appear in your cell.

2. Now move back up the column, one cell at a time. Make sure to look at each formula in the formula bar.

3. Finally, try editing one of your formulas. When you're in the right cell, click inside the formula bar. Then, make your changes, and press **Enter** to save them.

Easy, right? Just wait—it gets better.

The order of operations

There's no reason to limit your formulas to working with one operator. In fact, you can string together a formula that's as long as you want. Here's an example of a complicated formula that does many different mathematical operations:

```
=12+43*3-2^2+60/3
```

When you mix-and-match operators, you need to be aware that Excel won't just calculate the formula from left to right. Instead, it follows the mathematical rules called *order of operations*. Here's the order it uses:

1. Calculate stuff in parentheses (brackets)

2. Calculate exponents

3. Perform multiplication and division (from left to right)

4. Perform addition and subtraction (from left to right)

In the previous example, there aren't any brackets, but there are exponents, multiplication, division, addition, and subtraction. Here's an expanded look at how Excel calculates the formula, one step at a time:

```
=12 + 43 * 3 - 2^2 + 60 / 3
=12 + 43 * 3 - 4 + 60 / 3
=12 + 43*3 - 4 + 60 / 3
=12 + 129 - 4 + 20
=157
```

Controlling the order with brackets

If you have a complicated or long formula, you might lose track of the order of operations. If you're in doubt, or if you just want to make your formula clearer, you can add brackets (also known as *parentheses*). Putting stuff inside brackets is a little like getting into a priority line at Disney World. When Excel evaluates a formula that has brackets, it does the stuff inside the brackets first.

Imagine you timed your morning commute on five different days during the week. Your commute took you 44, 50, 45, 44, and 38 minutes. Now you want to figure out the *average* commuting time. You might try to get the answer from Excel with a formula like this:

```
=44+50+45+44+38/5
```

But there's a problem. Because of order of operations, Excel will divide 38 by 5, and then add that to your other commuting times, which isn't what you want. Fortunately, one set of brackets can put things right:

```
=(44+50+45+44+38)/5
```

Now Excel adds all your commute times and divides the total by 5. (The answer, should you try this for yourself, is 44.2 minutes, which is a long time to spend on the road. We hope you have audiobooks.)

Excel is notoriously picky about brackets. If you open a pair of brackets then you better be sure to close it later in your formula. If you don't Excel will catch the problem and insist you fix it before allowing you to move on to another cell.

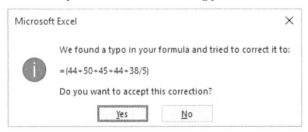

Advanced formula writers can put one set of brackets inside another (and another, and another), but be careful. Usually it's a better idea to break really long formulas into several smaller formulas, and connect them together with cell references. You'll learn to use this technique in the next chapter.

Exercise #1: Pocket calculator Excel

If your eyes are starting to glaze over from staring at other people's formulas, it's time to write a few of your own.

Head to the tutorial site, http://lab.halfwit2hero.com/excelformulas and check out the "Pocket calculator" workbook. It describes several mathematical calculations and asks you to write each one in Excel's formula language. When you see the right result appear on your worksheet, you'll know that Excel did your calculation correctly.

Formula Mistakes

It's easy to make a minor mistake that sidelines a formula.

For example, you might add an extra brackets, or accidentally type something that makes no gosh darn sense, like =5+*2 (5 plus times 2?) or =4^ (4 to the power of nothing in particular?)

These mistakes are called *syntax problems*, and Excel catches them immediately. Excel won't let you leave a broken formula in your worksheet. Instead, it asks you to fix the problem and even provides a possible correction you can use.

Sometimes, you'll write a formula that is syntactically correct but produces an error when Excel tries to evaluate it. This problem is more common when you start pulling information in from other parts of your worksheet and adding fancy functions—techniques you'll learn later. But you can see one example if you defy your high-school math teacher and attempt to divide by zero:

=42/0

Math nerds know that this isn't solvable. (Technically, the answer is "undefined.") Excel tries to explain the problem by showing an error code in the cell.

Error codes always start with the # symbol. The code `#DIV/0!` means "Whoops, you tried to divide by zero!"

A cell that has a formula error also gets a little green triangle in the top-left corner. If your worksheet has a bunch of mistakes, these triangles let you spot them easily.

When you move to a cell that has an error, Excel pops up a handy error icon (an exclamation mark in a diamond). If you click the error icon, Excel shows a more descriptive error name (like "Divide by Zero Error") and gives you a few more options:

▶ **Help on this error** pops up the Excel help window, which tries to explain what this error code means, using the sort of language a robot might use when talking to a calculator. (Don't expect it to be much help.)

▶ **Show Calculation Steps** shows a special window where you can watch Excel solving your formula, one step at a time. This window isn't useful right now, but if you have a complex formula that draws on information throughout your worksheet, it can help you find out what part of the formula went bad.

▶ **Ignore Error** tells Excel to stop showing you the green triangle for this cell, because you don't care about this problem. The error code that's in the cell stays put.

▶ **Edit in Formula Bar** has the same effect as just clicking in the formula bar, where you can edit the broken formula and make it work again.

▶ **Error Checking Options** brings up a page of Excel settings where you can choose to ignore certain types of errors, or just change the color of Excel's green error triangles. Unless you're an expert, there's no reason to tweak these details.

Most of these choices are overkill. If you have a bad formula, you can just click up in the formula bar and fix the problem yourself.

Unmasking Your Formulas

One thing that can cause confusion when you start learning about formulas is the way they lurk behind the scenes. When you look at a worksheet, all you see is a bunch of text and numbers. You can't tell (at least not at a glance) where your formulas are placed. You can go to each cell and peek in the formula bar, but that takes time, and it forces you to look at each formula separately.

But Excel has a nifty trick that can yank the curtain back and expose *all* your formulas at once. To try it out, open a workbook that has at least one formula (but preferably more). Then, choose **Formulas** ▷ **Formula Auditing** ▷ **Show Formulas**. (Depending on the size of your Excel window, Excel might not show the "Show Formulas" caption on the button. If you don't see it at first, look for a tiny picture with the "15/fx" symbol.

Hover over that, and you'll see the words "Show Formulas" pop up, confirming you've got the right button.)

When you click **Show Formulas**, Excel does two things. First, it doubles the width of every column on your worksheet, so you have more room to read formulas. Second, it shows every formula *on your worksheet*, right inside each cell.

So if you start with a worksheet like this:

▲	A	B	C	D	E
1					
2		JAN-APR	MAY-AUG	SEP-DEC	Total
3	Starting Balance	$1,500.00			Total
4	Total Income	$0.00	$0.00	$0.00	$0.00
5	Total Expenses	$0.00	$0.00	$0.00	$0.00
6	Net Difference	$0.00	$0.00	$0.00	$0.00
7	End Balance	$1,500.00	$1,500.00	$1,500.00	
8					

When you click **Show Formulas**, you'll get this:

▲	A	B	C	D	E
1					
2		JAN-APR	MAY-AUG	SEP-DEC	Total
3	Starting Balance	1500			Total
4	Total Income	=B15	=C15	=D15	=SUM(B4:D4)
5	Total Expenses	=B32+B43+B53+B59+B116+B	=C32+C43+C53+C59+C116+C	=D32+D43+D53+D59+D116	=SUM(B5:D5)
6	Net Difference	=B4-B5	=C4-C5	=D4-D5	=SUM(B6:D6)
7	End Balance	=B4-B5+B3	=B7+C4-C5	=C7+D4-D5	
8					

In this example there are plenty of formulas to check out. For example, look at cell B7. In normal view it shows the formula result, which is the number $1,500. In formula view it shows the formula that does the work, which is =B4-B5+B3

Formula view doesn't damage your worksheet—it's temporary. To get back to normal, just click **Show Formulas** again. When you do, Excel tucks your formulas back out of sight and shrinks all your columns by half, getting them back to their original sizes.

Itching to try this out for yourself? You can use this trick on the "Pocket calculator" workbook from the exercise earlier in this chapter. Give it a whirl!

Pro tip: If you really want to impress ordinary people, learn the secret **Ctrl+`** shortcut. It lets you trigger the **Show Formulas** command without lifting your fingers from the keyboard. The trick is to find the right key. It's not the ordinary apostrophe, but the mysterious "accent grave" key (also known as the "backtick"). On a standard keyboard, you can find it to the left of the number 1 key, near the top-left corner of your keyboard. It shares space with the equally exotic tilde (~) character. Once you've found the right key, hold down **Ctrl** and press this key to show or hide your formulas instantly.

If you want, you can even *print* your worksheet o' formulas. Just use the standard **File** ▷ **Print** command while you're in formula view. However, you'll probably want to resize your columns beforehand. Shrink the columns that don't have formulas, so you aren't wasting paper with blank space. Expand any columns that still aren't wide enough to show your formulas, so your printout has the full calculations. But be warned, if you resize your columns in formula view, you'll need to resize them again when you switch back to normal.

The Last Word

You've now taken one step into the world of Excel formulas. You wrote a few formulas that use basic math, saw their results, and learned how to edit them. You then got a bit fancy by learning to spot formula mistakes and expose an entire worksheet of formulas at once.

Right now, your formulas don't have much pizzazz. But in the next chapter you'll take a big leap forward. You'll learn to pull information out of the cells in your worksheet and weave it into your formulas. Read on to learn how.

Using Cell References

"The answer is in your worksheet. But first you must tell Excel where to find it."

So now you know what an Excel formula is, and how to write one. The problem is that the formulas you've used so far aren't terribly useful.

That's about to change. In this chapter you'll take the next big step—you'll learn to pull numbers out of other cells in your worksheet and use *them* in your formulas. This sounds like a small detail, but it changes everything. It means that instead of using Excel like a glorified pocket calculator, you can use it to analyze your own information. Even better, when you edit your worksheet, your formulas will adjust themselves to use the new numbers. It's like magic! Read on to see how it works.

Referring to Another Cell

It's easy to grab a value from another cell. Just type the equal sign (=) to start a formula, and then type the *cell address*. Here's an example:

=B1

This formula tells Excel "look for cell B1 and copy its value into my formula." If cell B1 has the number 26 in it, the result of this formula is, unsurprisingly, 26.

Now consider this formula:

=B1+B2

When Excel evaluates this formula, it gets the numbers in cell B1 and cell B2, adds them together, and shows the result. Where does the result appear? Wherever you've put the formula, of course.

A quick refresher on cell addresses

To be comfortable with Excel, you need to get comfortable with cell references.

Each cell address is a label that points to a single cell in Excel's grid. The first part of the cell address is a letter that identifies the column (like B) and the second part is a number that identifies the row (like 2).

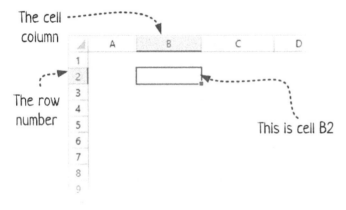

For example:

▶ The cell address B2 points to the cell in column B, row 2.

▶ The cell address F2 points to a cell in the same row 2, but farther to the right, in column F.

▶ The cell address B100 points to the one hundredth cell in the B column.

Chapter 3: Using Cell References

If you aren't sure which cell you're in, Excel can help you out. Look in the small white box that appears at the top-left corner above the worksheet grid. The address of the current cell appears there. (And if you want some extra practice using cell addresses, check out the "Find the cell" practice exercise from Chapter 1, which is on the tutorial website.)

The #VALUE! error

Excel expects numbers in your formula. If you try to use a cell that has some text in it, your formula won't work. For example, there's no way to add 432 and "Pajama party."

You'll know that one of your cell references has text in it if your formula shows the error code #VALUE! instead of a proper result.

Interestingly, there's no rule against using blank cells. In a formula, Excel treats a blank cell as though it has the number 0 in it.

Try it out: Point-and-click formulas

The straightforward way to add a cell reference is to type it in. But if you're having trouble remembering the exact cell address, there's another way. You can simply *click* the cell you want to use while you're building your formula.

Here's how this trick works:

1. Press the equal sign (=) to start your formula.

2. Now click the cell that has what you want. (If you accidentally pick the wrong one, just click again on the right one.) Excel highlights the cell you clicked and adds a reference for it to your formula. Here's what it looks like if you start a formula in cell D2 and then click cell B2:

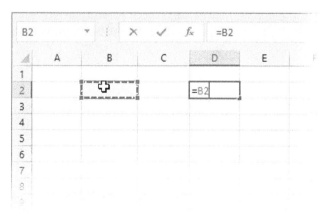

3. Keep typing in your formula. For example, if you want to add a number from another cell, press the plus sign (+) and click *that* cell. Excel will add the matching reference to your formula.

4. When your formula is perfect, press **Enter** to finish it.

Exercise #1: Calculate the sales tax

To see how useful cell references can be, you need to try a more realistic example. On the tutorial website (http://lab.halfwit2hero.com/excelformulas) there's an example that invites you to calculate the total cost of a fancy new smartphone, with tax included.

Here you start with the list price. It's up to you to write a formula that grabs the list price (using a cell reference) and calculates the tax. You'll then build on this with another formula (and another cell reference) to calculate the total cost. Before you go any further, try it out.

Cell references are alive (sort of)

Here's the nifty thing about cell references: they never go out of date. When you change the number in a cell, Excel notices. It instantly recalculates any formulas that use the cell.

It's easy to try this out using the "buy a smartphone" example. Simply edit the cell that has the cost of the phone. When you press the **Enter** key to make your change, Excel updates the result of the tax-calculating and total-calculating formulas to reflect the new price.

This flexibility is what makes cell references so useful. Imagine you create a worksheet that calculates the total cost of something more complicated—for example, a computer with lots of parts, or a home renovation. Later, you can change any number, and Excel will update *all* the formulas that are affected.

Remember, you can format your answer

When you write a formula that uses cell references, Excel tries to guess what formatting you want for the result. For example, if you're adding two Currency values (numbers that have dollar signs and two decimal places), Excel assumes the answer should use the Currency format as well. But if that's not what you want, you can pick a different format, in the same way that you pick a format for any other cell.

If you've forgotten how to pick the format for your cell, just remember it's all in the ribbon. First, move to the cell. Then, click the **Home** tab and look in the **Number** section. There you'll see a handy list of format choices you can pick from, and extra options for adding or removing decimal places, commas, and currency symbols.

Copying Formulas

A typical Excel worksheet doesn't have just one formula. It doesn't have just two. It could easily have a dozen or more.

Often, many of these formulas are similar to each other. In this situation, Excel has a feature that can save you some serious time. Instead of forcing you to write a dozen versions of the same formula, Excel can take one of your formulas and create copies that are tweaked *just right* so they work with different cells.

Try it out: Copy a formula

To see how Excel's formula copying feature works, start by writing a formula in a workbook. This formula can be as simple as you want, as long as it uses at least one cell reference. Here's an example with a basic formula that adds two cells in a row:

⬜	A	B	C	D
1				
2	5	10	=A2+B2	
3	12	3		
4	19	6		
5	26	11		

Now it's time to copy your formula. Follow these steps:

1. Move to the cell that has the formula.

2. Press **Ctrl+C** to copy the formula.

3. Move to a different cell and press **Ctrl+V** to paste your copy.

Chapter 3: Using Cell References   **49**

4. Now, look at the formula in the formula bar. You'll notice that Excel didn't copy the formula exactly. Instead, it *changed* the cell references.

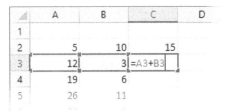

So what happened? Just as you shifted your formula to a new position, Excel shifted all the cell references to match. Move your formula ten rows down, and Excel shifts all the cell references down ten rows, too. And if you move your formula two columns to the right, your references go with it, two columns to the right.

Exercise #2: Copy a calorie formula

It's easier to understand how Excel's formula copying feature works if you do it yourself. The "Calorie counter" exercise gives you a good place to practice. It starts out with a spreadsheet that totals up the calories in different meals.

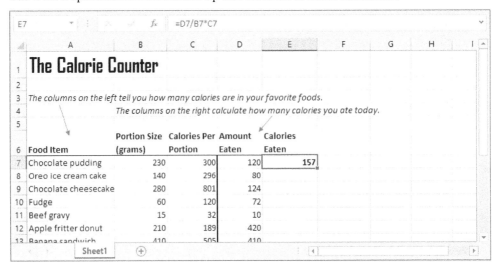

At first, the calorie counter has just one formula, in cell E7. This formula calculates how many calories you've eaten of a specific food—in this case, chocolate pudding.

The formula works by dividing the amount you ate (D7) by the portion size (B7) to find out the number of portions you ate. It then multiplies that by the calories per portion (C7) to find out the total number of calories you consumed:

=D7/B7*C7

This formula gets all its information from the cells in the same row. (This is a common arrangement. Formulas often use the numbers beside them in the same row, or the numbers above them in the same column.)

Here's closer look at how this formula gets its information:

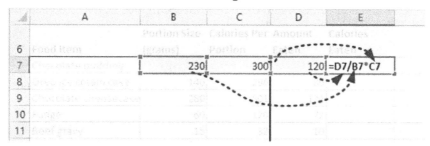

To calculate the amount of calories in the next item on the list (Oreo ice cream cake), you need a similar formula:

=E8/B8*C8

This is basically the same formula, but for row 8 instead of row 7.

Now, you *could* type the right formula for each food item. But that takes time, and there's a chance you'll make a typo along the way that will result in a difficult-to-spot calculation error. Copying the formula is much quicker, because it gets Excel to make the adjustments you need. Try this example on the tutorial site at http://lab.halfwit2hero.com/excelformulas.

Relative references and fixed references

Technically, the cell references you've seen so far (like A1 and E4) are *relative references*. That means they depend on the position of your formula.

Excel also allows you to create *fixed references*. Relative references and fixed references behave exactly the same, except if you copy your formula. When copying, Excel adjusts the relative references but it doesn't adjust the fixed references.

To use a fixed reference, just add a dollar sign ($) in front of the column letter and another one in front of the row number.

For example, you could change this relative reference:

=A4

to this fixed reference:

=$A$4

Both references point to cell A4 (and both have exactly the same effect in your calculation). The difference is that Excel won't change the fixed reference ($A$4) if you copy the formula to another cell.

A formula can have a mix of relative and fixed references. In fact, that's often exactly what you need. The following exercise demonstrates why.

Exercise #3: Copy a calorie formula (again)

When you copy a formula and Excel adjusts the references, it seems a little like magic. But sometimes this adjustment makes a reference point to the wrong cell.

To see this problem in action, consider a different version of the calorie counter worksheet:

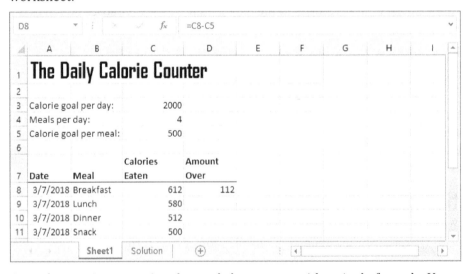

As in the previous exercise, the worksheet starts with a single formula. You need to copy this formula (in cell D8) to the cells underneath.

The problem is that the calorie-calculation formula in this example draws on cells that are in different places. The "calories eaten" cell is in the same row as the formula. The "calorie goal" cell sits above the table, in cell C5.

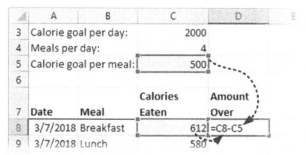

The calorie goal is the same for every formula, so every copy should use cell C5. But when you paste a copy of the formula, Excel adjusts it to point to a different cell. This messes up your calculation.

You may already see how you can solve this problem with a fixed reference. Head to the tutorial site (http://lab.halfwit2hero.com/excelformulas) to work through the solution.

Mixed references

Along with relative references and fixed references, Excel supports another type of reference.

You can make a *mixed* reference by adding just *one* dollar sign ($). For example, if you use reference $A4, the column is fixed but the row is not. When you copy the formula, Excel can change the row (for example, to $A5 or $A7) but not the column. Similarly, if you use the mixed reference A$5 in a formula and copy it, Excel can change the column letter but not the row.

Mixed references are less common than relative references and fixed references, but we thought you should know about them. You'll get to use them when you work through the "Make me a millionaire" exercise in Chapter 6.

Referring to Cells in Other Sheets

So far, you've used references to point to different cells on the same worksheet. This is the most popular type of reference. But Excel lets you reach out even farther, to cells that are in other worksheets.

A quick refresher on worksheets

Before you go any further, here's a quick recap about worksheets and workbooks. Every *workbook* (that's the official name for an Excel file) starts with a single work*sheet*. But you can add as many worksheets as you want.

There are plenty of reasons to add more worksheets. For example, imagine you're running a catering company. You can create a workbook that has two worksheets. On one, you put the list of all the food and services you offer, and their prices. On the other worksheet you can total up the cost of everything your client wants for their next party. Neat, right? (You'll see how to create this example in Chapter 10.)

At the bottom of the Excel window, there's a tab for each worksheet. A new workbook has one worksheet, named Sheet1.

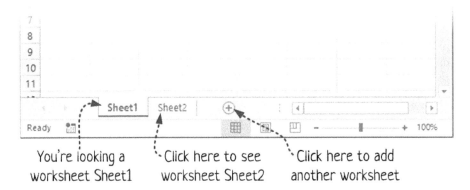

You're looking a worksheet Sheet1   Click here to see worksheet Sheet2   Click here to add another worksheet

To add a new worksheet, click the plus (+) button. If you've never done it before, try it out now.

You can add as many worksheets as you want, but once you get more than four or five the list of tabs starts to get crowded. Of course, you can only *see* one worksheet at a time. Click a worksheet tab to switch from one sheet to another.

Here are a few more things you can do with worksheets:

▶ **Rename a worksheet.** Names like Sheet1 and Sheet2 don't mean much. To pick something more descriptive (like Sales or Catalog) right-click the worksheet tab, choose **Rename**, and type in a better name.

▶ **Change the order.** To rearrange your worksheets, click a worksheet tab and drag it to the left or to the right, while holding down the mouse button.

▶ **Delete a worksheet.** If you don't want to a worksheet any longer, right-click the worksheet tab and choose **Delete**. Excel won't let you delete all the worksheets in your workbook, because that wouldn't make sense, would it?

▶ **Copy a worksheet.** Sometimes you need several worksheets with the same basic layout. To create a quick worksheet copy, right-click the worksheet tab and choose **Move or Copy**. Then check the **Create a copy** checkbox and click **OK**.

▶ **Hide a worksheet.** You can make a worksheet disappear temporarily. Right-click the worksheet tab and choose **Hide**. (When you want it back, right-click any worksheet tab, and choose **Unhide**.) Right now, you probably can't think of any good reason to hide worksheets, but it in can be useful if you're sharing a workbook with lots of different people, and you want to tuck some of the details out of the way.

Worksheet references

As you already know, you refer to another cell like this:

`=A1`

This formula grabs the value from cell A1 in the current worksheet (the worksheet where you're typing the formula).

But what if you want to grab the value from cell A1 in a *different* worksheet?

It's easy. Just put the workbook name, followed by an exclamation mark (!), followed by the cell address. For example, if you cell is in a worksheet named Sheet2, you would write this:

`=Sheet2!A1`

And here's a formula that adds the numbers from cell A1 and cell A2, both of which are on Sheet2:

`=Sheet2!A1+Sheet2!A2`

There's one catch. If the worksheet name has a space in it, you need to wrap the whole name in apostrophes ('). So if your worksheet has the name Product Catalog, you would need to refer to it like this:

`='Product Catalog'!A1`

If you make a mistake in the sheet name, Excel won't be able to find what you want. Instead of getting a proper result, you'll see the error code `#REF!` appear on your worksheet.

Try it out: Referring to another worksheet

Now's a good time to try this out for yourself. Here's how:

1. Create a new workbook. Like all workbooks, it will start with a single worksheet, named Sheet1.

2. Add a new worksheet to your workbook by clicking the plus (+) button. Excel names the new worksheet Sheet2.

3. In Sheet2, pick a cell (any cell), and type in a number.

4. Click Sheet1 to switch back to your first worksheet.

5. Type = to start writing a formula in Sheet1. Now you're going to add a reference to your cell in Sheet2.

6. You could type the reference in by hand. But a quicker approach is to use Excel's point-and-click formula feature. While you're editing your formula, click the Sheet2 tab and then click the cell that has your number in it.

7. Click back to Sheet1. You'll see that Excel has added the Sheet2 reference to your formula.

8. Add to the formula if you want, or just press **Enter** to finish up.

Workbook references

Referring to a cell in another worksheet is super-useful. Excel also allows oyu to referring to a cell in another workbook file, which is less useful and a lot more risky.

The problem is that there's no way to make sure your files stick together. If one workbook file points to another, what happens when you email that workbook to a friend or move it to another folder? (Spoiler alert, the workbook won't be able to find the cell it needs any longer, and you'll be stuck with out-of-date information.)

But if you really must create a workbook reference, there's only one good way to do it—use the trusty point-and-click formula method. Here's how:

1. Open both workbooks at once.

2. Press = to start a formula in one workbook.

3. Switch to your other workbook and click the cell you want to reference.

4. Switch back to the workbook where you're writing the formula and keep going. (Or, just press **Enter** to switch back and finish the formula in one step.)

Here's the sort of reference Excel will create:

```
='[Price list.xlsx]Sheet1'!$B$8
```

When you add a reference to a cell in another workbook, Excel includes the file name in square brackets (Price list.xlsx), the sheet name (Sheet1), and the cell address as a fixed reference ($B$8).

This is actually a simplified version of the real reference. As soon as you close the workbook that you're referencing (in this case, that's "Price list.xlsx"), Excel will update your reference with the full file path. Your formula will change into something like this:

```
='C:\Users\joemascapone\My Documents\[Price list.xlsx]Sheet1'!$B$8
```

That's a loooong formula for a single reference. It's a hot mess.

If you ignore our advice and use workbook references, and your references break because you've moved or renamed your files, all is not lost. Excel will notice the problem and ask you to pick the file you're trying to reference. Once you do that, your references will be reconnected. (You can also look at all the linked files your workbook uses—and change them—by choosing **Data** ▷ **Queries & Connections** ▷ **Edit Links**.)

Tracing References with Arrows

You've now learned everything you need to know about cell references. In fact, you're ready to skip on to the next chapter and start tackling the next stage of formula writing. But if you have a spare moment, it's worth taking a quick detour to learn about a nifty Excel trick called *tracing arrows*.

The idea is simple. When you use tracing, Excel temporarily draws arrows on your worksheet to point out important relationships. There are two types of relationships you can see:

▶ **Precedents.** These are the cells that a formula uses to make its calculation. If you have the formula =A1+A2 then A1 and A2 are precedents.

▶ **Dependents.** These are the formulas that use your cell. For example, if you're positioned on cell B3, every cell with a formula that uses B3 is a dependent.

The best way to understand this precedent/dependent jargon is to see it for yourself, in action, with Excel's tracing feature.

Try it out: Tracing the calorie counter

The sample exercises in this chapter are a great testing ground for tracing, because they all have formulas that use cell references. Here's how you can get started exploring the calorie counter:

1. Open the "Calorie Counter 2" workbook that you used in the third exercise. If you have your completed copy on hand, use that. If not, you can grab the starting workbook from http://lab.halfwit2hero.com/excelformulas (there's a link in the first step of the third exercise) and switch to the Solution tab.

2. Move to cell D8, which has the "Amount Over" calculation for the first row in the table.

---

3. Click **Formulas** ▷ **Formula Auditing** ▷ **Trace Precedents**. The effect is immediate. You'll see two arrows that show the relationships: the formula in cell D8 uses cells C5 and C8:

4. You don't need to stop your investigation just yet. If you click **Trace Precedents** again Excel digs one level deeper. It adds arrows to show you what your dependent cells use:

In this example, C8 doesn't use anything, so it doesn't get any arrows. But C5 has its own formula that uses cells C3 and C4, so you get two more arrows there.

These arrows are a bit harder to see, because Excel draws them one on top of the other.

5. You could go to another cell (like D9) and find its dependents, too. There's no limit to how many arrows you can draw on your worksheet at a time. When you're finished, click **Formulas** ▷ **Formula Auditing** ▷ **Remove Arrows** to clear the arrows off your worksheet.

6. Now let's try tracing dependents. Move to cell C5.

7. Click **Formulas** ▷ **Formula Auditing** ▷ **Trace Dependents**. Excel finds all the cells that use C5 in a calculation and draws an arrow to each one:

As you can see, there are eight cells that use C5.

In this example, your tracing didn't uncover anything unexpected. But tracing can become very useful when you need to investigate errors and figure out where a failed formula is getting its bad data.

You might have noticed that tracing arrows are the second formula auditing feature that you've seen. In Chapter 2, you looked at the **Show Formulas** button, which is in the same **Formulas** ▷ **Formula Auditing** section of the ribbon. You'll learn about one more formula auditing feature in Chapter 5—that's the **Evaluate Formula** button that lets you watch Excel crunch the numbers in any one of your formulas.

The Last Word

Cell references are one of the most important ingredients in Excel formulas. They let you write formulas that use the information on your worksheet—*your* information.

In this chapter, you learned to write cell references. You also learned how Excel adjusts relative references when you copy them (and how you can tell Excel to lay off with fixed references). Finally, you created long-armed formulas that reach out to gather their information from other worksheets.

Using Functions

"Smart people solve hard problems. But a genius gets someone else to do the work."

So far you've learned to write straightforward formulas that do their work with Excel's arithmetic operators (the symbols for addition, subtraction, division, and so on). But Excel is way smarter than that. To unlock its real power, you need to use *functions*.

A function is a special sort of calculation that Excel will do for you. For example, Excel has a function that automatically calculates square roots. If you want to get the square root of a number, you don't need to write a formula for that on your own—instead, you can ask Excel's function to do the work.

Some Excel functions are simple (like the square root one), and some are ridiculously complicated. Excel has specialized functions for engineering, statistical math, and financial analysis. In this chapter, you'll learn how to use Excel's functions in your formulas.

Adding a Function to a Formula

The easiest way to learn how to use an Excel function is to start with an example. We'll use Excel's square root function, which is named SQRT. (Every Excel function name is written in uppercase letters. It's like a toddler shouting for your attention.)

To use a function, you need a formula. So find a cell and hit the equal (=) key to start one. Then, type the function name, like this:

```
=SQRT
```

This formula isn't finished yet. After every function, you must place a pair of brackets:

```
=SQRT()
```

Depending on the function you're using, the brackets might be empty, or you might need to put something inside. The information you put inside the brackets is sent to the function, which uses it to perform its calculation.

In the case of the SQRT function, you *do* need to add something in the brackets. Excel needs to know what number to get the square root of. For example, if you want to find the square root of 9, use this:

```
=SQRT(9)
```

Now your formula is finished. (Spoiler alert: the result of this formula is 3, because 3×3 is 9.)

Instead of using a number, you can use a cell reference with the SQRT function—or with any function, really. For example, if you want Excel to grab the number that's in cell B1 and calculate *its* square root, you'd write this formula:

```
=SQRT(B1)
```

There's nothing that stops you from creating more complicated formulas that combine functions with other calculations, or use more than one function. For example, this formula finds the square root of 9 and adds the square root of 4:

```
=SQRT(9)+SQRT(4)
```

If you're wondering how this affects Excel's order of operations, which you studied in Chapter 2, here's the simple answer

▶ First, Excel evaluates each function in your formula, working from left to right.

▶ Next, Excel does all the mathematical operations in its usual order (brackets, then exponents, then multiplication and division, and finally addition and subtraction).

Function parameters

There's a technical name for the information you put inside a function's brackets: *parameters*. The SQRT function uses a single parameter, but some functions need more information.

For example, consider the ROUND function, which rounds a number to the precision you choose. It needs two parameters: the number you want to round, and the number of decimal places to keep.

When you have a function that needs more than one parameter, you use a comma to separate each parameter. So if you want to take the number 413.768 and round it to two decimal places, you can use this formula:

`=ROUND(413.768, 2)`

In this example, there's a space after the comma, before the second parameter. That space is optional, but it makes the two parameters are easier to read. The result of this formula is 413.77

The order of parameters is important. Switch them around, and you won't get the right answer. Fortunately, Excel helps you out a bit by showing you *hints* while you type your formula. You'll see what we mean when you try it out in the next section.

Try it out: Putting a function in a formula

Now it's time for you to use your first function.

1. Here's the setup. Start a new, blank workbook. Then, in cell A1, type a number with some decimal places to it, like 312.4934

2. Move to another cell (any will do) and press the equal (=) sign to start your formula.

3. Type the first "R" in ROUND. Right away, Excel understands what you're trying to do—use a function. It shows a help list with all the functions that start with R.

4. Type the rest of the word ROUND. Or, if you're too lazy to move your fingers that much, you could just click ROUND in Excel's list. (My favorite shortcut is to keep typing letters until ROUND shows up at the top of the list—in this case, by the time you get to U—and then press the **Tab** key to get Excel finish the function name.)

5. Now it's parameter time. Type the opening bracket first. Once again, Excel's eager to help you. It shows you how many parameters you need, and names each one.

Sometimes it's a bit tricky figuring out what the parameter name is supposed to mean, but in this case it's pretty straightforward—the *number* you want round and the *num_digits* (number of digits) you want to round it. If you see a parameter name wrapped in square brackets—like [*num_digits*]—that parameter is optional. Depending on what you're trying to do, you may be able to leave it out.

6. In this example, you want to round the number that's in cell A1. So use the cell reference A1 for the first parameter. Pick the number of digits you want for the second parameter. Here's what you need to round the value in A1 to have no decimal places:

   =ROUND(A1, 0)

7. Press **Enter** to finish your formula and take a look at the rounded result.

A quick aside about rounding

You might remember that you can also use Excel's number formatting features to round numbers. For example, if you have a number with too many decimal places, you can use the **Decrease Decimal** button from the **Home** ▷ **Number** section of the ribbon.

Here's the difference. When you use number formatting, you change the way a number *looks* on the worksheet, but you don't change the number. When you use the ROUND function, Excel calculates the rounded number and swaps that in place of your original number. Usually, this difference is no big deal. But if you want to do more calculations with your rounded numbers, it can have an effect. (For example, if you add three rounded numbers together, you may get a different answer than if you add three unrounded numbers and then round the result. Yeah math!)

Errors that can attack your formulas

Even the best formula writers run into problems every once in a while. You'll know your formula has messed up if you see an error code, like #VALUE! instead of an answer.

Most errors are easy to fix. Here's a quick rundown of the error codes you might see when using ordinary functions, and the most common reasons they occur:

▶ #NAME? appears when Excel can't figure out what function you're trying to use. For example, if you write ROND instead of ROUND, or you forget to include the brackets after your function name, you'll get this error.

▶ #VALUE! usually means you've given a function the wrong type of data. For example, if you try to use ROUND with a cell that has text in it, you'll see this bad boy.

▶ #REF! tells you that there's a problem with one of your cell references. For example, if you have a formula that uses cell B3 and you delete the entire column B (right-click the column header and choose **Delete**), this error appears in your formula. It's Excel's way of warning you that your formula is no longer pointing to what you think it is. To fix the problem, edit the formula and put in the right reference.

▶ #NUM! usually means your formula has broken down in the face of an impossible calculation. Possible offenses include calculations that result in staggering large numbers (anything with more than 309 digits), or trying to find the square root of a negative number.

▶ #DIV/0! is a problem that occurs when a formula attempts to divide by zero. You can make this mistake even without functions.

▶ #N/A! is a lookup error that tells you Excel can't find the data you want. You won't encounter this error until you use the lookup functions in Chapter 10.

Sometimes errors occur through no fault of your own, even in perfectly good formulas. For example, a divide-by-zero error can happen when you're missing some information. In Chapter 9, you'll learn some tricks to avoid errors (or at least hide them) with conditional functions. But in the simple formulas you're using right now, an error usually means you made a mistake that you can fix with a quick formula edit.

Excel's Function Library

As you saw, Excel is eager to help you out wherever it can. Not only does Excel help you figure out your function parameters, it can also help you look up a function that you need.

Excel has over 400 functions (although lots of them overlap and some are old fashioned functions that have been replaced by newer, better versions). One way to start digging through this huge pile functions is to go to the **Formulas** tab in the ribbon. There, in the **Function Library** section, are several function lists. Each list is themed around a certain type of function. For example, if you click **Math & Trig**, you'll see a list of functions that can help you do high school math (for example, calculate factorials, sines, cosines, lowest common denominators, pi, and so on).

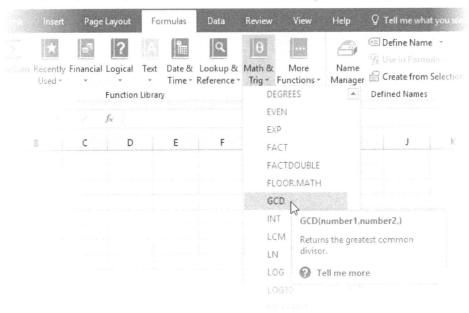

If you see a function that looks interesting, hover over it for a moment with the mouse pointer. Excel will show you a short description.

In the example here, Excel explains the GCD function, which looks at a list of numbers and gives you the largest whole number that can divide all of them, without leaving a remainder. The "Tell me more link" looks inviting, but it isn't much help. It loads the Excel function reference, which attempts to explain every Excel function using highly technical Excel-ese language.

Putting one function inside another

If you want to be really tricky, you can even put one function *inside* another. Check it out:

```
=SQRT(ROUND(80.9, 0))
```

When Excel evaluates this formula, it starts with the innermost function, ROUND(80.9, 0). Then it takes the rounded answer (81) and passes that to the outer SQRT function to get the answer, 9.

Reading this kind of formula can get confusing, because it's easy to miss a bracket. If you want, you can add spaces to make it clearer where each function is placed:

=SQRT(ROUND(80.9, 0))

Now here's an example that switches the order around and puts a SQRT function inside a ROUND function:

=ROUND(SQRT(7), 2)

In this example, Excel calculates the square root of 7 first (which is something like 2.64571) and then rounds that result to two decimal places (2.65).

There's no limit to how crazy you can get putting one function inside another. In fact, you can put *many* layers of functions inside each other, like a set of wooden Russian dolls that nest inside each other.

Sometimes you can avoid nesting by breaking a big calculation down into multiple steps and doing each step in a separate cell. In the previous example, you could calculate the square root of 7 in one formula, and then write another formula that takes the result from that cell and rounds it. But there are good reasons to use at least some nesting, so you'll see it crop up every once in a while—including in the next practice exercise.

Exercise #1: Princess of trig

Using functions isn't hard. But learning about all the different functions Excel has, and learning how to use them, can take time.

This rest of this book shines the light on some Excel's most useful functions. But before you go any further, now's a good time to practice using a function. On the tutorial site (http://lab.halfwit2hero.com/excelformulas), there's a "Princess of trig" worksheet that invites you to use trigonometry to find how out long Rapunzel's hair should be.

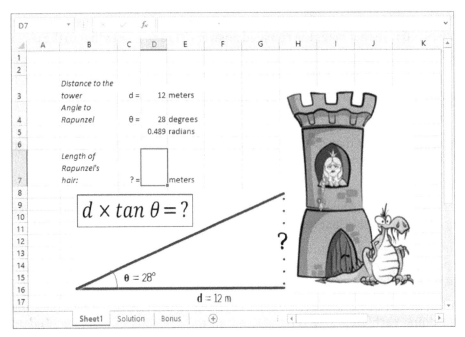

Don't worry, you don't need to figure out the math. The exercise gives you the equation that provides the answer. But you *do* need to find the right function and use it to get your answer.

Try it out: Excel's handy conversions

Once you get comfortable putting functions in your formulas, you'll face the real challenge—finding the function you need and figuring out how it works. In the previous exercise, you tried your hand at trigonometry. Now, you'll practice with a completely different function.

Excel's function library has more than a few hidden gems. One of them is the CONVERT function, which converts numbers from one measurement unit to another. For example, the CONVERT function can change a distance measured in miles to the equivalent in meters, yards, Picas, parsecs, or light years. The CONVERT function can't convert *everything*, but it does know how to handle an impressive variety of units for distance, weight, area, volume, pressure, temperature, speed, force, and more.

To try out the CONVERT function, let's calculate the number of teaspoons of Coke in a standard 2 liter bottle. The CONVERT function needs *three* parameters—that's the most you've seen so far. Here's the full formula:

```
=CONVERT(2, "l", "tsp")
```

The first parameter is the number you want to convert (in this case 2, for 2 liters). The second and third parameters are special codes that indicate measurement units.

Chapter 4: Using Functions

The second parameter sets the current measurement unit ("l" for liters) and the third parameter sets the new measurement unit you want to use ("tsp" for teaspoons). Notice that the codes ("l" and "tsp") are wrapped in quotation marks. This is the rule for using text in a formula. If you leave out the quotation marks, Excel thinks you're trying to use a nested function named l or tsp, which won't work.

The result, roughly 405.8, tells you how many teaspoons of Coke fit in the bottle.

The trick to using CONVERT is finding the right codes for your units. Here's where Excel is ready to help. To see how, try typing the formula in. You'll get this far:

```
=CONVERT(2,
```

As soon as you type the comma, Excel will pop up a list of all the codes it knows. All you need to scroll through the list and click the one you want.

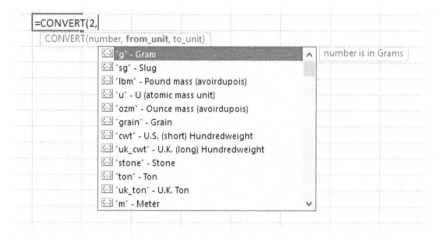

Even better, once you pick a code and enter the next comma, Excel offers you a shortened list of conversion choices. For example, if you pick a unit of distance for the second parameter, Excel shows you all the other distance units (but not units for other types of measurement).

Before you go on, take CONVERT for a test spin. It's a good example of an Excel function—it needs several parameters, it prompts you with possible values, and it gives you a useful answer at the end.

Functions that Use Cell Ranges

Imagine this: a function that doesn't look at just one cell, but grabs a whole *group* of cells. It's one of Excel's best tricks, and it lets you calculate sums, averages, and statistical distributions.

Adding numbers with SUM

One example is Excel's legendary SUM function. SUM has one job in life: to suck up a pile of numbers and spit out a total. And while you don't need to use SUM to add numbers, you're about to see why it's so useful.

Imagine you have a list of expenses:

You already know how to add these up with cell references. You could write a formula like this one:

`=B4+B5+B6+B7+B8+B9+B10`

This works, but it's long. And if you add another expense to your expense list, you'll need to edit your formula, which is a bit tedious and raises the very real possibility that you'll make a mistake. Leave out one of these cell references and your formula will still appear to work, but it'll give you the wrong number.

Wouldn't it be great if there was a function that could do the work more simply and more quickly? That's where SUM comes in.

When you use SUM, you give it a *group* of cells. In this case, the group starts in cell B4 and ends in cell B10. In Excel language, this is the range `B4:B10`.

Here's the formula:

```
=SUM(B4:B10)
```

When you type or edit this formula, Excel highlights the cells that are in the range using a shaded box.

	A	B	C
1	Shopping List		
2			
3	*Item*	*Cost*	
4	bananas	$ 4.13	
5	pyjamas	$ 12.50	
6	Tide PODS	$ 17.88	
7	chocolate chips	$ 1.99	
8	aspirin	$ 4.99	
9	lottery tickets	$ 25.99	
10	bread	$ 0.99	
11			
12	TOTAL:	=SUM(B4:B10)	
13			

The SUM function ignores blank cells and cells that have text in them. That means you can give SUM an extra-big range so there's room to add items to the shopping list. However, first you need to move the SUM formula out of the way so there's room for the list to grow. For example, you could put the SUM formula at the top of the list:

	A	B	C
3	TOTAL COST:	=SUM(B6:B18)	
4			
5	*Item*	*Cost*	
6	bananas	$ 4.13	
7	pyjamas	$ 12.50	
8	Tide PODS	$ 17.88	
9	chocolate chips	$ 1.99	
10	aspirin	$ 4.99	
11	lottery tickets	$ 25.99	
12	bread	$ 0.99	
13			
14			
15			
16			
17			
18			
19			

Now you can use a formula like this:

`=SUM(B6:B18)`

This range includes some extra blank cells. If you add more items later, you'll put the prices in these cells. The SUM function will grab them all and update the total, and you won't need to adjust your formula. And there's no reason to stop at cell B18. If you want to have space for a huge shopping list, you can extend the range right down to B100, B1000, or the bottom of the worksheet (cell B1048576).

More about ranges

To define a range, you use two cell addresses: one for the first cell in the range, and one for the last cell in the range. You can grab cells vertically (going down a column) or horizontally (going across a row).

If you use two cells in the same column, like B4:B10, Excel includes these two cells and the ones in between (B5, B6, B7, and so on). In this example, it grabs a total of seven cells.

If you use two cells in the same row, like B10:G10, Excel includes B10 on the left, G10 on the right, and everything in between (C10, D10, E10, and so on). This makes for a horizontal strip of six cells.

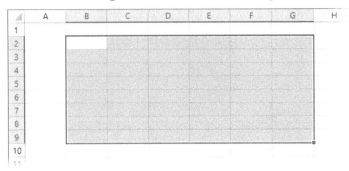

You can also grab a rectangular group of cells. This doesn't make sense for all functions, but it's indispensable for some. To define this type of range you need to tell Excel the cell at the top-left corner of the rectangle and the cell at the bottom-right corner. So the range B2:G9 makes this rectangle:

The SUM function works with rectangular ranges, so you can try this out for yourself. (However, you probably won't ever use a rectangular range with a SUM function in a real spreadsheet, because usually the numbers you want to add are in one column or one row. You *will* use rectangular ranges to grab whole tables of data with certain functions, like the lookup functions in Chapter 10.)

Selecting a whole column (or row)

It's often handy to select an entire column of cells. You could do using a range like B1:B1048576, but Excel has a shortcut. Just use the column letter with no row number, like this:

=SUM(B:B)

This formula totals up all the non-blank cells in column B.

You can also grab more than one column at once, by using the starting column letter and the ending column letter, like this:

=SUM(B:D)

This grabs all the cells in columns B, C, and D.

The same trick works to select an entire row. Just use the row number with no column letter. This formula sums up the contents of row 3:

=SUM(3:3)

Or here's one that gets rows 3 and 4:

=SUM(3:4)

The SUM function ignores text, so it's safe to use this formula on cells that include headings, titles, or descriptive text. However, the SUM function doesn't ignore dates (it converts them into numbers, as you'll learn in Chapter 5), so don't let them slip into your cell range.

One final note: if you want to add up an entire column, make sure you put the formula that does it in a *different* column. (The same goes for adding up a row—put the formula in a different row.)

Imagine what happens if you put a formula that sums up column B in cell B1. The formula attempts to total the whole column, *including itself*, which doesn't make much sense. Try it, and Excel will warn you that you've created a *circular reference*, which is Excel's fancy way of describing a formula that refers to itself. When you have a circular reference, Excel won't evaluate the formula that's causing the problem—you'll just see a useless answer like 0.

More functions that like ranges

The SUM function is an old Excel standby, but Excel has plenty of other functions that work with ranges. Here are some of the most useful:

▶ COUNT counts how many cells there are with numbers or dates in them. Text doesn't count. You can also use the COUNTBLANK function to count blank cells, or the COUNTA function to count how many cells there are that aren't blank (meaning they have numbers, dates, or text).

▶ AVERAGE calculates the average value out of a group, ignoring blanks and text cells just like SUM.

▶ MAX finds the biggest number in a group. MIN finds the smallest, and MEDIAN gets the one that's in the middle.

All these functions are known as *statistical functions*. Statistics is the branch of mathematics that deals with collecting and analyzing large samples of data. Excel has several bucketloads of statistical functions, which you can browse by clicking **Formulas ▷ Function Library ▷ More Functions ▷ Statistical**.

Unless you have an advanced math background, you aren't likely to use most of Excel's statistical functions. (Quick test to see if you are: would you like to find the confidence interval for a population mean using a Student's T distribution? Yes, Excel's got a tailor-made function just for that.)

Even if you aren't a statistics nerd, you're likely to use the simpler statistical functions in the list above. You'll try them out in the next exercise.

Exercise #2: Take the temperature

The best way to get cozy with ranges and the functions that use them is to try them out on a sample worksheet. The "Take the temperature" worksheet on the tutorial site (http://lab.halfwit2hero.com/excelformulas) has you covered. It provides two lists of temperature measurements made during the month of July in New York city. There are some missing measurements in the data, but that's no challenge for Excel's statistical functions.

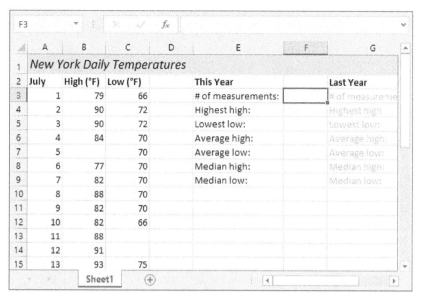

Using the functions you just met, you can analyze this information and compare it the previous year. Give it a go!

The Last Word

Functions are the secret sauce in an Excel formula sandwich. They let you do everything from counting a list of numbers to "returning the inverse of the left-tailed probability of the chi-squared distribution." (That's the CHISQ.INV function, if you're wondering. Unless you're a statistician, you're not interested.)

In the rest of this book, you'll meet some of Excel's most famous functions. Each one does something different, but they all work the same basic way. You put the function in a formula, set some parameters, and use the result. And armed with functions, there's very little you can't do.

Calculations with Dates and Time

"Today is the tomorrow you worried about yesterday."

When someone says "check out this formula," most people expect to see numbers. But Excel is just as good at calculations that use dates and times.

For example, a simple date calculation is "how many days until my birthday?" A more complicated date calculation is "how many days have I lived on the planet?" Excel can answer both questions with nothing more than a subtraction sign.

Excel also has a toolbox of date functions that can solve trickier problems, like "what day of the week does my birthday fall on in 2020?" and "how many workdays are there this February?" In this chapter, you'll learn how to answer all these questions, with no need to consult a calendar.

Unmasking Excel Dates

Excel pays attention to what you put in your worksheet. So far, you've been filling your cells with bits of text and numbers. But in this chapter, you'll start stuffing your cells with dates.

To type in a date, you use one of Excel's recognized date formats. Here are the three most common choices:

▶ 15-Jan-19

▶ 2019-1-15

▶ 1/15/2019

After you type in a date, it's easy to double-check that Excel recognizes it. Just move to the cell and look in the formula bar. No matter what the date looks like on your worksheet, in the formula bar Excel uses the standard short date format that's set for your computer. On computers with U. S. regional settings, that's 1/15/2019.

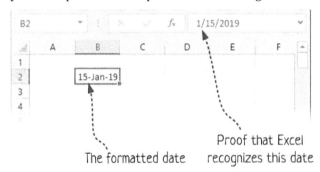

The formatted date   Proof that Excel recognizes this date

Date formatting

Dates are just like numbers: you can change their appearance by changing their formatting.

The two most common date formats are in the format list, in the **Home ▷ Number** section of the ribbon. They are the short date format that you just saw, and the more verbose long date format, which includes the day of the week and looks like this:

Tuesday, January 15, 2019

These two formats obviously don't tell the whole story. Excel gives you a much wider range of ways to present a date. To see some more of Excel's date formats, choose **More Number Formats** at the bottom of the format list.

This pops open a Format Cells window with more number formats. Click **Date** (in the leftmost list) to see more than a dozen formatting choices for dates.

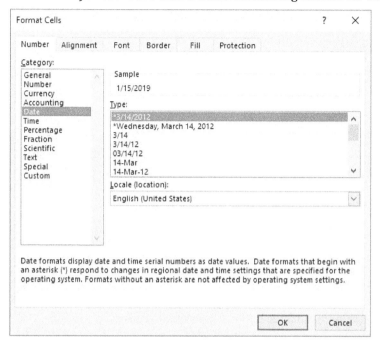

You'll find some formats that don't show the year information (like 1/15 or 15-Jan). You'll find a long date format that doesn't include the day of the week and even some date formats that include the time of day (more on that later). But remember, no matter what you pick, Excel stores the same date information in your worksheet. If you don't display the year, Excel still keeps track of it, and the correct year reappears if you change back to a date format that uses it.

Pro tip: If you aren't satisfied with Excel's date formatting choices, you can build your own personalized date format. We aren't going to explore that feature, but if you're curious Excel has the step-by-step instructions at http://tiny.cc/exceldate

Try it out: Peeking at date numbers

Here's a dirty Excel secret. Behind the scenes, every Excel date is actually a number. Excel doesn't even try that hard to hide this reality. To see for yourself, follow these steps:

1. Type a date into a cell (let's say cell A1). Use any date you want (for example, try 1/15/2019).

2. Click the cell.

---

3. Using the format list in the **Home** ▷ **Number** section of the ribbon, pick **General**. You'll see your date transform into a five-digit number, like 43480.

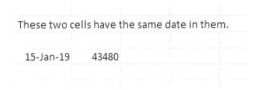

These two cells have the same date in them.

15-Jan-19   43480

That's right. Every date is really a number. Technically, this date-as-a-number is called a *serial number*, and it counts how many days have elapsed since January 1, 1900. So if you see the number 43480, it means that 43480 days have elapsed since January 1 in the year 1900. (If you have a lot of free time and a stack of calendars, you can confirm that this eventually leads to January 15 in the year 2019.)

The smaller the serial number, the older the date is. If you want Excel to recognize a date *before* 1900, you're out of luck. It's date numbering system doesn't support dates that old, so Excel will treat your date like an ordinary piece of text.

The date numbering system isn't just an Excel quirk. Because dates really *are* numbers, you can use them in formulas just like you would use ordinary numbers. As you'll see in the next section, this makes date calculations very easy.

Basic Date Math

Because dates are numbers in disguise, you can do everything you do with numbers to dates. But what does it mean to add something to a date, or subtract one date from another? Read on to learn the meaning behind the math.

Adding days to a date

You can add two dates together. But you won't, because the answer doesn't actually mean anything.

What you might do is take a date and add a number of days to it. For example, if you put today's date in cell C2, here's a calculation that tells you what date it will be in 100 days:

```
=C2+100
```

This formula works because it takes the number that represents the current date (like 43480) and tacks on some extra days (100, to be precise). This shifts the date forward.

You can also use subtraction to move a date backward in time. Here's how you'd take a date and move it 30 days into the past:

```
=C2-30
```

When you use date addition or subtraction Excel always find the correct calendar date. You don't need to worry about how many days are in a month, or whether you're passing through any leap years. Excel takes care of all these details.

When you add days to a date or subtract days from a date, the answer is always another date. Every once in a while, Excel will get confused and display the result (the new date) as an ordinary number (like 43580). For example, this might happen if you already applied a number format to the cell that has the date formula.

Fortunately, fixing this problem is a simple matter of Excel formatting. First, go to the date cell. Then, in the **Home** ▷ **Number** section of the ribbon, choose one of the date formats from the format list.

Start date:	1/15/2019
Add days:	100
Answer formatted as a number:	43580
Answer formatted as a date:	4/25/2019

Finding the difference between two dates

Although it doesn't make sense to add two whole dates together, it does make sense to subtract one date from another. If you do, you get the number of *days* between those two dates. This works whether the dates are close together (say, in the same month) or far apart (separated by years or even centuries).

For example, if you put the current date in cell B2, and the date of your next birthday in cell B3, this formula tells you how many days you need to wait until cake day:

```
=B3-B2
```

This is a simple formula, but it's useful in plenty of different circumstances. Want to know how long you've been on a job? Put today's date in cell B3 and your start date in cell B2. Want to know how long you've been alive, in days? Put today's date in cell B3 and your birth date in cell B2. Just remember, the *newer* date always comes first in the formula, and you subtract the *older* date.

When you use this format, you don't need to apply any extra formatting. That's because the result is a number of days, not a date. It makes perfect sense to see the result as an ordinary number.

Getting today's date

The TODAY function is one of Excel's simplest date functions. You put it in a formula, and it grabs the current date.

Here's an example:

=TODAY()

Even though the TODAY function doesn't use any parameters, you still need the brackets after its name. Otherwise, Excel doesn't know you're trying to use a function and you'll get the infamous #NAME? error in your cell.

The TODAY function always shows the current date—that's the date it is right now when you're looking at the worksheet (not the date that you wrote your formula). So if you save your workbook and open it tomorrow, you'll see a different date appear.

The TODAY function is also handy in date calculations. For example, if cell A2 has your birthday, this is the number of days you've been alive so far:

=TODAY()-A2

There's one quirk. This formula calculates a number of days, but Excel wants to show it as a date, so you'll get a nonsensical result like 5/8/1938. To fix this problem and switch back to a normal number, go to the cell, look at the format list in the **Home** ▷ **Number** section of the ribbon, and choose **General**.

Writing a date in a formula

Take another look at Excel's standard short date format:

> 1/15/2019

As you already know, when Excel looks at this date it sees a single number. But you can also treat a date as a combination of three pieces of information: the month number (in this example, 1), the day number (15), and the year number (2019).

Excel has a DATE function that lets you create a date out of these month, day, and year numbers. For example, if you write this formula:

=DATE(2019,1,15)

Excel generates the date number 43480. If your cell uses date formatting, you'll see the date 1/15/2019 appear on your worksheet.

The DATE function is handy if you want to plop a date right in the middle of a formula, without using a cell reference. Here's an example that calculates the number of days between the present day and Neil Armstrong's moon landing on July 20, 1969:

```
=TODAY()-DATE(1969,7,15)
```

This is a lot easier than figuring out the date number for this historic event (it's 25399, if you were wondering), and putting that in your formula.

Another approach is to put the moon landing date somewhere on your worksheet. You could then insert it into your formula with a cell reference. In fact, this is often the most convenient approach. But sometimes, the DATE function makes life simpler and keeps worksheets from getting too cluttered. It's also an important ingredient in the more advanced date calculations you'll see shortly.

Taking a date apart

You just learned how to assemble a date out of three pieces information. Excel also lets you take a date apart using three functions: DAY (to get the day number), MONTH (to get the month number), and YEAR (you know what it's for).

Here's an example of a formula that uses the MONTH function:

```
=MONTH(B3)
```

Assuming you've put a date in cell B3, the result is a number from 1 to 12, representing that date's month.

The Date:	9/12/1921
MONTH:	9
DAY:	12
YEAR:	1921

The obvious question is "Why do you want just part of a date?" The answer is because it allows you to do different types of date calculations. Instead of just adding and subtracting days, the DAY, MONTH, and YEAR functions let you add and subtract whole months or years at a time. You'll see how to do that in the next section.

Moving a date by months or years

Imagine you want to take a date and shift it exactly one month into the future. You might try a formula like this:

```
=B2+30
```

But this is an approximation. Some months have more days and some have fewer.

A better approach is to use the MONTH function, which gives you the month number for a date, and add 1.

```
=MONTH(B2)+1
```

This formula doesn't solve the problem (yet). It increases the month number, but it doesn't create a whole date. The challenge is to use the new month number to make a new date. For that, you need to take the new month number and all the other date details, and give them to the trusty DATE function.

Here's a formula that does the trick:

```
=DATE(YEAR(B2), MONTH(B2)+1, DAY(B2))
```

This formula uses the magic of nested functions. It uses the YEAR, MONTH, and DAY functions to get the year, month, and day information from the date in cell B2. Then, it changes the month number by adding 1. And finally, it passes all that information to the DATE function so it can create the new date you want.

If you got lost in this sequence of events, don't worry! The next section lets you see how this formula works, one step at a time.

Pro tip: This calculation moves the date forward exactly one month. So if you start with a date on January 15, Excel moves it to February 15. You can add as many months as you want, even if it makes the month number larger than 12. Excel just moves the date into the next year. (There's one exception. If you try to move to a date that doesn't exist, like February 30, Excel rolls the date over to the next month.)

Try it out: Watching Excel calculate a date

To start this experiment, create a new worksheet and write a date in cell B2. The actual date doesn't matter (our example uses 1/15/2019).

Next, move to cell B3. In cell B3, write this formula:

```
=DATE( YEAR(B2), MONTH(B2)+1, DAY(B2) )
```

You don't need to add the spaces (Excel lets you add spaces in a formula wherever you want, but they don't affect the calculation). But you *do* need to pay close attention to the brackets. Leave one out, and Excel complains immediately.

You'll know you wrote the formula correctly when you see a date appear in your cell. This is the date that falls one month after the date in cell B2. If you used January 15, 2019 for your start date, the formula result is February 15, 2019.

Here's where life gets interesting. You can watch live as Excel does its formula evaluation. This is a great way to understand complex formulas that use nesting. Just follow these steps:

1. Make sure you're on the cell with the formula (cell B3).

2. In the ribbon, choose **Formulas** ▷ **Formula Auditing** ▷ **Evaluate Formula**. Excel opens the Evaluate Formula window, where it shows the step-by-step process it uses to evaluate the current formula.

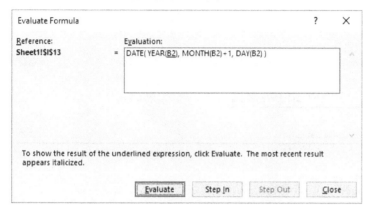

3. Click the **Evaluate** button to make Excel evaluate one part of the formula and then pause. You'll see Excel grab the date for the first cell reference, changing the YEAR(B2) part of the formula to something like YEAR(43480).

4. Click **Evaluate** again to make Excel evaluate the next part. Now you'll see Excel evaluate the part of the formula that has the YEAR function, replacing YEAR(43480) with the actual year (like 2019).

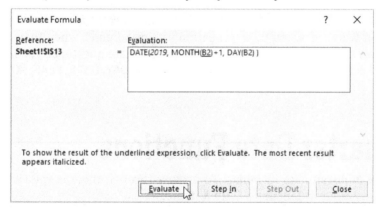

5. Keep clicking the **Evaluate** button until Excel has finished evaluating the whole formula. At this point the **Evaluate** button changes to **Restart**.

6. Click **Restart** to watch the steps all over again, or click **Close** to get back to your worksheet.

Exercise #1: The new hire

You've covered a lot of ground with Excel's date calculations. Here's an exercise (available at http://lab.halfwit2hero.com/excelformulas) that gives you the chance to practice your date math.

This worksheet records some important dates for a company's newest employee. Using the start date as a jumping off point, it's up to you to calculate how long the employee has been working, when their probationary period ends, when their first performance review takes place, and more. To solve these date questions, you'll use date math and the essential date functions you just met: TODAY, DATE, YEAR, MONTH, and DATE.

Even Smarter Date Functions

Excel has a couple of dozen date formulas. To browse through them in the ribbon, choose **Formulas** ▷ **Function Library** ▷ **Date & Time**.

Some of Excel's date functions are specialized tools that won't interest most people. (For example, the DAYS360 function performs date calculations using an odd system that pretends every month has exactly 30 days. It's designed for use with certain types of accounting calculations, and it doesn't make sense for ordinary date math.) But many of Excel's more exotic date functions can be quite useful. You'll try the most useful ones in the following sections.

Finding the day of the week

You've already seen how you can pull day, month, and year information out of date. But what if you want to know the *day of the week*? Excel's got you covered with the WEEKDAY function.

Using WEEKDAY is easy. You give it a date and it gives you a number from 1 to 7, where 1 represents Sunday, 2 represents Monday, and so on. Here's an example that gets the day-of-the-week number for the date in cell B3:

```
=WEEKDAY(B3)
```

So if you get 3, the date falls on Tuesday.

Using the WEEKDAY function you can get plenty of interesting information. For example, why not find out what day of the week your 85th birthday falls on, so you can start party planning?

Counting workdays

If you have a regular 9-to-5 job, you know that days come in two flavors: weekdays and weekends. Excel's date functions have no trouble telling the difference.

One of these functions is WORKDAY. It takes two parameters: a starting date and the number of workdays you want to count forward. For example, let's say you buy a new sofa online and they tell you it will be delivered in 10 business day. Here's how you would find the delivery date:

```
=WORKDAY(TODAY(), 10)
```

This function takes the current date (using TODAY) and counts 10 days forward, skipping over Saturday and Sunday. So if you start on January 15, 2019, the formula counts ahead to your delivery date, January 29, 2019.

Today:	12-Aug-18
10 workdays later:	24-Aug-18

There's a quirk here. Even though the result is a date, Excel won't automatically apply the date format to the cell, so you'll see a number like 43494 instead of your date. To fix this issue, choose a proper date format from the **Home** ▷ **Number** section of the ribbon.

Excel also has a NETWORKDAYS function that counts the workdays between two dates. Here are the workdays between today and a project deadline, which is stored in cell C2:

```
=NETWORKDAYS(TODAY(), C2)
```

Chapter 5: Calculations with Dates and Time

Of course, weekends aren't the only reason not to work. There are also holidays, which Excel ignores. (In Excel's workaholic eyes, even Christmas is a workday.) If you want to use holidays in your workday calculations, you need to add a list of holidays to your worksheet. You can then use your holiday list with the WORKDAY and NETWORKDAYS functions.

For example, imagine you have a list of holidays in cells D4 to D20. When you call WORKDAY and NETWORKDAYS, you need to tell Excel about these holidays. To do that, you add an extra parameter that has the cell range with your dates:

```
=NETWORKDAYS(TODAY(), C2, D4:D20)
```

Now NETWORKDAYS won't count any of the dates that you've designated as holidays.

Or if you're really fancy, you can have a whole column of holidays in a separate worksheet, like this:

```
=NETWORKDAYS(TODAY(), C2, Holidays!A:A)
```

This gets all the dates in the A column in a worksheet named Holidays. For a refresher on using references to point to different types of ranges and separate worksheets, flip back to Chapter 4.

Finding the end of the month

The end of the month is an important date. Schools and businesses use it to set deadlines and make payrolls.

Excel has a helpful EOMONTH function that can find the end of any month. For example, this formula finds the date for the end of the current month:

```
=EOMONTH(TODAY(), 0)
```

The second parameter, 0, tells EOMONTH to look at your date and find the end of the month. If you use a different number, EOMONTH counts forward that number of months, and then finds the end of *that* month. (Yes, it's a bit weird, but accountants often use EOMONTH to look ahead and find future month-end dates.)

Remember to apply a date format to the cell that uses the EOMONTH formula, or you'll see a date number instead of a readable date.

And here's a bonus—a fancy formula that fuses together NETWORKDAYS and EOMONTH to count how many work days are left before the end of the current month:

```
=NETWORKDAYS(TODAY(), EOMONTH(TODAY(),0))
```

Calculating your age

Here's a surprisingly tricky question. How do you use an Excel formula to calculate someone's age based on their birth date?

You might think you could use simple date subtraction. So assuming the birth date is in cell A2, you would write this:

```
=TODAY()-A2
```

This gets you the number of *days* a person has been alive. But this doesn't tell you their age in *years*.

You could try dividing the answer by 365, but this won't always work because leap years can mess you up. (The older the person is, the more leap years accumulate, and the worse the problem gets.)

The solution is Excel's YEARFRAC function. It gets the *exact* proportion of years for a given number of days. If YEARFRAC is 1, that means you have exactly one year's worth of days. Usually, that means 365 days, but if you're in a leap year Excel is smart enough to use 366 days.

Here's how you can use the YEARFRAC function to make an age calculation:

```
=YEARFRAC(A2, TODAY())
```

In this example, YEARFRAC starts by calculating a number of days between the current date and the birth date in cell A2. It then converts this to a fractional number of years. If you're 24 years old and your birthday is around the corner, YEARFRAC might give an answer like 24.82.

Of course, no one describes themselves as being 24.82 years old (even if it is accurate). Instead, you're 24 years old until you reach your birthday, at which point you jump straight to 25.

To get the true no-decimals-allowed age from YEARFRAC, you need to get rid of the extra numbers. But formatting alone can't do the trick, because if you tell Excel not to show the decimal places it will round your age up to 25, which isn't right either. For the same reason, the ROUND function isn't any help.

What you really need is a function called ROUNDDOWN, which chops off all decimal places. If you give ROUNDDOWN a number like 24.82, it hands you back the number 24.

Using ROUNDDOWN, you can create an age-calculating formula that never goes wrong:

```
=ROUNDDOWN( YEARFRAC(A2, TODAY()) )
```

Birthdate:	1/18/1989
Today:	1/12/2018
Age with ordinary math:	29.003 (ignores leap years)
Age with YEARFRAC:	28.983
Age with TRUNC and YEARFRAC:	**28**

How Excel Sees Time

Not only can Excel work with dates, it can also work with *times*. This probably comes as a surprise, because you don't often see a time value show up in a worksheet (and you haven't seen any in this book so far). But using time is easier than it seems.

In fact, Excel recognizes several short time formats, just like it recognizes short date formats. For example, if you want to type in the time 3:45 PM, you can do it using any of these formats:

▶ 3:45 PM

▶ 3:45:00 PM

▶ 15:45

It's up to you whether you want to show hours, minutes, and seconds, or just hours and minutes. One important detail is to remember that if you don't tack on a space and the letters "PM" Excel uses a 24-hour clock. So if you type in just 3:45 Excel assumes you are referring to 3:45 AM, which might not be what you want.

Time formatting

Just like dates, times are actually numbers behind the scenes. But while dates use whole numbers, times use *fractional values*—numbers less than 1.

To unmask 3:45 PM, go to the cell and apply the General number format. Here's what you'll get:

0.15625

Every time is a fractional value somewhere between 0 and 1. For example, 0 represents 12:00 AM midnight at the very start of the day, and 0.5 is exactly halfway through the day, at 12:00 PM.

There's a reason for this odd system. Because dates use whole numbers (like 43480) and times use decimal numbers (like 0.15625), you can combine the two to get a date and time information in a single cell. For example, the number 43480.15625 means 3:45 PM on January 15, 2019.

Math with times

As you've probably guessed, you can do calculations with time values. For example, you might want to add an hour to a time, or find the number minutes between two time values, But because times are fractional values, the numbers you use aren't as straightforward as you might expect.

For example, check out this formula:

```
=A2+0.1
```

Assuming cell A2 has a time measurement, this formula adds exactly two hours and twenty four minutes. That's because according to Excel's fractional time system, 0.1 is 10% of a whole 24-hour day.

Adding a single hour or minute is messier, because you'll be forced to use odd fractions with lots of decimal places. No one really wants to write this:

```
=A2+0.000694444444444444
```

Fortunately, Excel gives you the TIME function that can do the conversion for you. When you use TIME, you supply a number of hours, minutes, and seconds (in that order). For example, here's how you can use the TIME function to add a single hour to a time:

```
=A2+TIME(1,0,0)
```

In cell A2 has the time 3:45 PM, this result of this formula is 4:45 PM.

And here's a similar formula that looks at a number in cell B2, and adds that number of minutes to the time in cell A1:

```
=A2+TIME(0, B2, 0)
```

So if A2 has 3:45 PM and B2 has 12 in it, the formula result is 3:57 PM.

A time:	3:45 PM
Add this many minutes:	12
New time:	3:57 PM

If you see a fractional result instead of a time, your cell has the wrong format. To fix this problem, go the format list in the **Home** ▷ **Number** section of the ribbon and choose **Time**.

Calculating intervals of time

So far, when you've seen a time value, it's been a *time of day*. But in some situations, you want to calculate the *total amount* of time.

Imagine you're trying to figure out how long it takes you to run a half marathon race. You put your start time in one cell (let's say B2). You put your finish time in another (B3). Now, you use a formula to calculate the difference:

=B3-B2

Perfect, right? Not quite. The problem is that Excel doesn't know how to display the result. If you use the standard time format you've been using so far, Excel assumes that your race running time is actually a time of day. So instead of saying you made it in 2:34:15 (two hours, thirty-four minutes, and 15 seconds), Excel thinks you mean the time of day 2:34 AM.

Start time:	7:15:00 AM
Finish time:	9:49:15 AM
Race time?	2:34:15 AM

Fortunately, this problem is easily solved if you follow these steps:

1. First, go to the cell with your formula.

2. In the format list in the **Home** ▷ **Number** section of the ribbon, scroll to the bottom and choose **More Number Formats**.

3. Now, you need to pick a format that's designed for time *intervals*, not the time of day. In the Category list on the left, click **Custom**.

4. Scroll down until you find the peculiar looking **[h]:mm:ss** format. Click to select it.

   The **[h]:mm:ss** is a code that tells Excel how you want your cell formatted. It tells Excel to show the number of hours, then the number of minutes, and then the number of seconds. The square brackets around the **[**h**]** tell Excel to calculate the *total* number of hours, even if you have more than a day's worth. So if you're measuring something that is 26 hours long, Excel thinks of it as being 26-hours long, not 1 day plus 2 hours.

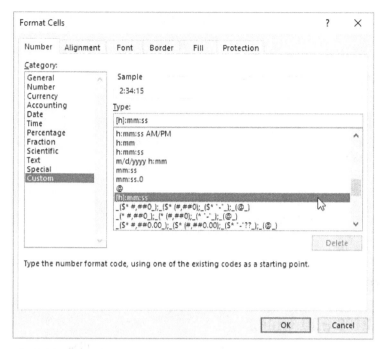

5. Click **OK** to update your worksheet.

Pro tip: Excel experts sometimes make their own time formats. For example, the format **[mm]:ss** isn't in the list, but you can type it into the Type box at the top of the list in the Format Cells window. This format tells Excel to show an interval time as a total number of minutes (so 2 hours and 24 minutes is displayed as 144 minutes). Microsoft has the full details for you at http://tiny.cc/customtime.

Exercise #2: Timing your commute

Now that you've learned to do math with times, it's time to try a realistic example. The "Clock the commute" exercise asks you to measure the time of daily trip to work (get it at http://lab.halfwit2hero.com/excelformulas). You also get to use the traditional AVERAGE function, which works with times just like it works with any other number.

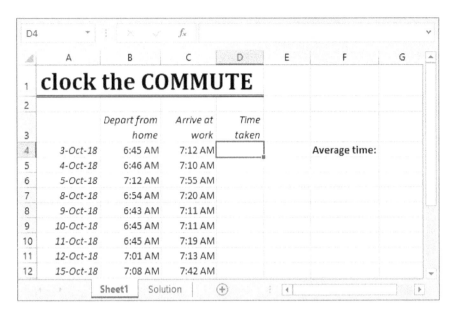

Combining dates and times

Excel is perfectly happy keeping dates and times separate. You can fill some cells with dates and some cells with times and you'll never run into a problem. But every once in a while you might want to combine a date and time into one cell. To do that, use one of the short date formats, followed by a space, followed one of the short time formats. For example, try typing in something like this:

> 1/15/2019 3:45 PM

This represents the time of 3:45 PM on January 15, 2019. If you want to record the exact time of a specific event on a certain day, this is pretty useful. And you can always use formulas to split up the date and time information. (One way is to use the DAY, MONTH, YEAR functions to get date information and the HOUR and MINUTE functions to get time information out of your cell.)

Combined dates and times aren't that common, and this format doesn't appear in the ribbon's format list. However, you can apply this format to any cell by heading to the **Home ▷ Number** section of the ribbon and choosing **More Number Formats**. Then, in the Format Cells window, pick the Date category (from the list on the left) and scroll down until you see a date format that includes date and time information. Choose it and click **OK** to apply it to your cell.

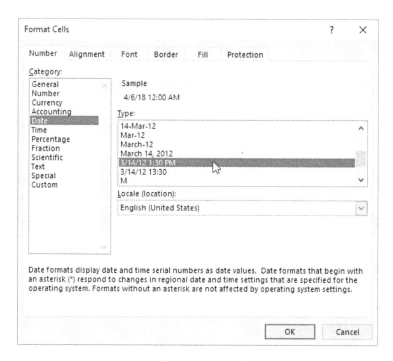

Getting the time (right now)

Excel has a NOW function that gets the current date and time. NOW is like the TODAY function you used earlier, except it includes time information.

```
=NOW()
```

The NOW function refreshes itself and gets the current time every time you open your workbook or evaluate another formula.

If you want the current time with no date information, just take away the date number for the current date. You can use this formula:

```
=NOW()-TODAY()
```

You'll need to apply the Time format to the cell that has this formula in it.

Here's a snapshot of the current day, the current day & time, and the current time all on its own:

TODAY:	3/23/2018
NOW:	3/23/2018 11:06 PM
NOW-TODAY:	11:06:12 PM

The Last Word

In this chapter, you learned the best-kept secret about Excel dates and times: they're really just numbers with a sprinkle of formatting sugar on top. And because they're numbers, you can put them in formulas and go crazy with calculations. Excel also has an impressive set of calendar-smart functions that can answer more complicated date and time questions.

This is the deal Excel offers: you put in the numbers, and it does the number crunching. As long as you know which functions to use, you don't have to do the hard work. In the next chapter, you'll use the same approach with formulas that work with money. As long as you give Excel the raw numbers, it provides the functions that help you budget for loans and plan your investments.

## Chapter 6

Calculations with Money

"The formulas agree: Mo' money, mo' problems."

There's nothing special about money in a worksheet. Amounts of money (also known as *currency values*) are just ordinary numbers with a bit of extra formatting. Any formula that works with numbers automatically works with money. So why do we need to talk about dollars and cents?

The answer is in Excel's function library. The people who made Excel also created a group of supremely useful financial functions. These functions can help you calculate investments, loans, and mortgages. In this chapter, you'll learn how to use them.

Excel's Financial Toolkit

Excel has a few dozen functions that every accountant loves. You can see them in the ribbon by choosing **Formulas** ▷ **Function Library** ▷ **Financial**.

Many of these functions are too specialized to interest anyone without a finance degree. For example, there are functions for calculating bond coupon dates, discounted treasury yields, and asset depreciation. We won't touch any of those.

However, there are a few financial functions that everyone should understand. They can help you answer questions like "How much interest am I paying on my loan?" and "How much should I save every month if I want to retire a millionaire?" These are the functions you'll use in this chapter.

Three key financial concepts

Excel's financial functions use some technical terms that can be a bit intimidating to ordinary, non-accountant people. Before you go any further, there are three financial concepts we should introduce:

▶ **Present value (PV)** is the value of an investment (or loan) at the beginning of its life. For example, if you put $1,000 in the bank, the present value is $1,000.

▶ **Future value (FV)** is the value of an investment (or loan) at some point in the future. Wait long enough, and that $1,000 in your account could grow to—well, probably not that much, actually. Maybe $1,012?

▶ **Rate** is the rate at which your investment or loan grows over time. For example, a savings account might pay you 1.2% per year, while a loan could charge you 6%, and a typical credit card demands a whopping 19.99%. (Yikes!)

Often, you'll have some of this information but not all of it. You can use a financial function to take the information you have and calculate what's missing. For example, if you know the starting value (PV) and the rate of an investment, you can predict its future value (FV)—what it will grow to in a couple of years. Or, if you have the starting value (PV) and future value (FV) of an investment, you can figure out what rate it earned.

The weird idea of negative money

Here's one weird detail you'll see with Excel's financial functions: negative money values (like -$3,000). No, this doesn't indicate an overdrawn account balance. Instead, it's a technique Excel uses to keep track of which way your money's flowing.

Here are the two rules Excel uses:

▶ If you're getting money, use a positive number. For example, if the bank lends you money or pays you some interest on an investment, that's positive. This is called a *cash inflow*.

▶ If money is leaving your hands, use a negative number. For example, if you're paying interest in a loan or putting money in an investment, you need to go negative. This can be a bit counter-intuitive, because if you but money in a savings account you aren't really *losing* it. You're just temporarily trusting the bank with its safekeeping. However, you still need to make the value negative so Excel knows the money is leaving your possession. This is called a *cash outflow*.

If you make a mistake, the financial functions will give you answers that don't make sense, like a savings account that decreases in value or a loan that grows bigger when you increase your monthly payments.

Seeing the Future

One of Excel's most famous financial functions is FV, which stands for *future value*. True to its name, the FV function looks ahead and tells you what an investment will be worth (or how much you'll owe on a loan) at some point in the future.

Calculating the growth of an investment

The FV function is designed for *fixed rate* investments—investments that promise to pay you a specific percentage of money every month. For example, you can go to your bank and buy a *certificate of deposit* (CD) that promises to pay you a fixed rate on the money you've saved. ("Certificate of deposit" is a term that's used in the United States. In other countries, banks offer similar products with different names—for example, GICs in Canada or fixed-rate bonds in the UK.)

Here's an example of a bank CD:

24-Month* Certificate of Deposit

5%
APY
(annual percentage yield)

THESE RATES WON'T WAIT!

*Penalties apply for early withdrawal

The deal is like this: you give the bank your money for two years. At the end of this period, the bank gives you back your money along with the extra interest it earned. But what this bank ad doesn't tell you is how much cash you'll have at the end.

This is where the FV function comes in. Here's a sneak preview of the formula that gives you the answer for a $3,000 deposit:

```
=FV(5%, 2, 0, -3000)
```

The result, $3,307.50, is the amount of money you'll have in two year's time (representing a tidy profit of $307.50).

rate:	5%
# of periods:	2
payment:	$0.00
pv:	-$3,000.00
FV function:	$3,307.50

To understand the FV formula, you need to understand its four parameters. Here are their shortened names:

```
FV(rate, number_of_periods, payment, pv)
```

You can probably figure out what some of them do just by name, but here's the complete breakdown:

▶ **rate (5%)**. The first parameter, the interest rate, is pretty straightforward—you're earning 5% each year, because that's what the bank promised you.

▶ **number_of_periods (2)**. The second parameter is the number of periods, which is a way of measuring how much time your money is invested. In this example, you're looking at an investment that pays you 5% every *year*, so the payment period is per year. You're investing for two years, so the number of periods is 2.

▶ **payment (0)**. The third parameter is the regular contribution you make each payment period (in this case, that's once each year). But because you aren't topping up your investment in this example, 0 does the trick.

▶ **pv (-3000)**. The money you're paying into the investment to start out ($3,000). This looks a bit wacky, because it's a negative number. Remember, when using the financial functions, you use negative numbers to represent money that's leaving your hands. The $3000 you give to the bank counts as money you're releasing.

This is one of the simplest examples of a formula with FV. Once you wrap your head around what each parameter means (and you get used to using negative money), it's not too difficult to understand.

Compound interest

In the previous example, the bank offered an *annual* rate of 5%. That means your interest is paid at the end of every year. But often your bank will pay your interest each month. For example, instead of giving you $300 at the end of year, your bank might pay you $25 each month.

Simple, right? Not so fast. If you're earning interest every month, that new money is flowing into your bank account throughout the year. And that small bit of extra money starts to earn a tiny bit of interest too. This effect is called *compound interest*—basically the extra interest you earn on the interest you've already been paid. The result is that you end up earning just a bit more money than you expected.

Here's an ad for a high-interest savings account that compounds monthly:

If you want to use FV to calculate the earnings on an investment that pays monthly interest, you need to make two adjustments.

First, you need to multiply the number of periods by 12. That's because the period is no longer once a year—now it's every month. If you're invested for two years, you'll pass 24 periods, because there's an interest payment each month:

=FV(5%, 2*12, 0, -3000)

Second, you need to divide the annual interest rate by 12. It would be great if your bank paid you 5% each month, but life is rarely so generous. Instead, each month the bank gives you a twelfth of the annual rate:

=FV(5%/12, 2*12, 0, -3000)

As this formula, your new total is $3,314.82. Thanks to monthly compounding, you now you earn about seven dollars more over the two years that you're invested.

year rate / 12:	0.4167%
# of years * 12:	24
payment:	$0.00
pv:	-$3,000.00
FV function:	$3,314.82

Technically, you get as much money from a 5% interest rate that's compounded monthly as from a 5.116% interest rate that's paid once per year. Excel even has a function that can figure this out for you, called EFFECT. You tell EFFECT the interest rate (5%) and the number of times your interest is being paid in a year (12 times for monthly interest). EFFECT tells you the equivalent annual interest rate:

```
=EFFECT(5%, 12)
```

The NOMINAL function does the reverse. You give it an annual interest rate, and it gives you an equivalent lower rate that will earn you just as much money if it's compounded monthly:

```
=NOMINAL(5%, 12)
```

Here's the formula gives you a result of 4.89%, because that rate with monthly compounding is just as good as a flat 5% annual rate.

Monthly compounding is very common with savings accounts. And it's essential with loans, because you make loan payments every month. Because monthly compounding is so common, you'll see plenty of formulas in this chapter that use it. Remember, you can tell that monthly compounding is at work when the formula divides the interest rate by 12 and multiplies the number of years by 12.

Exercise #1: An imaginary investment

Before going any further, you should try using the PV function to calculate the future of an investment. The "Imaginary investment" exercise on the tutorial site (http://lab.halfwit2hero.com/excelformulas) can help you out. It asks you to calculate the future worth of an unexpected inheritance from a dear old great-great aunt. On the way, you'll get a chance to compare two types of interest rates: compounded annually and compounded monthly.

Stocks and other investments

Asa you've learned, the FV function is designed to tell you how much money you'll earn from a *fixed rate* investment—an investment that has a set interest rate. For example, if your bank tells you that you're going to earn 2%, you can figure out exactly how much cash you'll have in the future.

But long-term investments (like retirement accounts) often put some of their money in stocks. The value of the stock market can fluctuate dramatically (especially in the short term), so there's no way to calculate how much money you'll have next week or next year. However, if you're using the FV function to imagine possible outcomes, there's no shame in making a reasonable assumption about how much you'll make.

Historically, the U.S. stock market has earned around 7% per year, if you average out the wild drops and climbs over a long period of time. Legendary investor Warren Buffet suggests that long-term investors can expect to make roughly 6% over the years. So if you use 6% with the FV function, you can make an educated guess about the future of your retirement savings.

Pro tip: If you're using FV to estimate what might happen to your stock market accounts, it's a good idea to use the calculation multiple times, with different rates. For example, you can calculate the future value with the rate you expect (probably 6%), and make a worst case scenario with a lower rate.

Paying a loan

So far you've looked at the future of an investment. The FV function works just as well at seeing what's in store for a loan. The main difference is how you use negative money.

With a loan, you start out by *receiving* money from the bank, so the present value (PV) in your calculation is always positive. But you also need to make monthly payments, and for that you use negative values.

For example, if you want to borrow $10,000 at 6.5% per year (compounded monthly), and the bank wants you to pay back $200 per month, here's the formula that tells you where you're at in four years:

```
=FV(6.5%/12, 4*12, -200, 10000)
```

Because your interest is calculated each month (and the payments are made each month), the rate is divided by 12 and the number of years of is multiplied by 12, just like you saw before.

Notice that the present value (PV) is positive, but the payment is negative. If you made the payments positive, it would mean that you're borrowing more money from the bank each month, and your loan balance would grow over time. The sad truth is money don't come for free.

The result of this formula is -$2,030.22, which is the amount still owing to the bank five years later.

rate:	6.50%
# of years:	4
payment:	-$200.00
pv:	$10,000.00
FV function:	-$2,030.22

Depending on the format you're using for your currency values, you might not see the negative sign in front of the result. For example, if you pick **Accounting** from the format list in the **Home** ▷ **Number** section of the ribbon, negative values get brackets around them and -$2,030.22 is shown as ($2,030.22).

Timing payments with the type parameter

The FV function (and many of the other financial functions you'll meet in this chapter) takes an optional parameter that you haven't used. That's the *type* parameter, which you can tack on after the other four parameters you already know about.

The type parameter must be either a 0 or a 1. (If you don't use the type parameter, it's the same as if you set it to 0.) A value of 0 tells Excel you're making your payments at the *end* of each payment period. So if you're paying monthly, the money leaves your hands on the last day of the month. But if you set type to 1, like this:

```
=FV(6.5%/12, 4*12, -200, 10000, 1)
```

Excel knows you're making payments at the *beginning* of each payment period. The effect of this change is that you'll make a little bit more money in an investment or pay off a loan just a little bit faster.

Answering More Money Questions

One of Excel's specialties is answering hypothetical questions. With investments, you might want to know how much money you need to put aside each month to meet a far-off goal, like retirement (or going on an electronic dance music cruise vacation). With loans, you might want to know when you'll clear your debt, or how your budget will change if interest rates double (be prepared to eat a lot of boxed macaroni). Either way, Excel's financial functions can run the numbers and help you plan for the future. They'll give you the good news—or a harsh wake-up call.

How much money do you need to save?

Here's a fun question: what do you need to do to become a millionaire?

To answer that question, you can invest in Excel's PV formula, which tells you the *present value* of an investment. This seems counter-intuitive—if you need to know how much something is presently worth, can't you just take a look at your most recent bank statement?

But PV is designed to work backwards. You give it some assumptions about the future, and it tells you what you need to start with in the present. For example, if you want to know how much you need to invest so you grow your investments to $1,000,000 dollars, you can play with PV to get some answers.

The PV function examples in this chapter use four parameters:

```
PV(rate, number_of_periods, payment, fv)
```

The PV function works a lot like the FV function you've already studied. The first three parameters (the rate, the number of payment periods, and the regular contributions you're making) are the same. The difference is the fourth value, which holds the future value you're trying to achieve.

Now imagine you're trying to make a million with a humble 5% interest rate. You're willing to wait 30 years. Here's the formula that tells you how much you need to invest:

```
=PV(5%/12, 30*12, 0, 1000000)
```

Notice that the 5% interest rate is divided by 12 because the investment is compounded monthly. You also need to multiply the 30 years of earning by 12 to get the total number of months you'll stay invested.

The formula answer is -$223,826.60. The negative number indicates that this is money you need to put into your investment. So if you have a spare $200,000 lying around and a lot of time to wait, it can grow into $1,000,000 without you touching it.

You'll have an easier time if you're willing to make regular payments. Let's say you put $550 aside each month. (Once again, this number will be negative in the formula because it's money leaving your hands.) Here's the revised calculation:

```
=PV(5%/12, 30*12, -550, 1000000)
```

Now your initial investment is reduced to about $120,000. That's still a lot of bank.

Don't give up quite yet. If you're an investment genius, maybe you can play the stock market and bring your earnings up to 8% a year. Here's a new calculation:

```
=PV(8%/12, 30*12, -550, 1000000)
```

Now you'll get there if you start with a modest $16,000 and change. Not so bad.

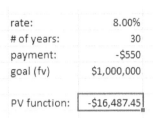

rate:	8.00%
# of years:	30
payment:	-$550
goal (fv)	$1,000,000
PV function:	-$16,487.45

Exercise #2: Make me a millionaire

One good way to compare different possible outcomes is to build a *two-variable table* in Excel. It allows you to compare dozens of slightly different financial calculations side-by-side, so you can see the effect of changing certain details.

This type of experiment is called a two variable table because you get to pick *two* pieces of financial data that can change (or *vary*). For example, in the tutorial site (http://lab.halfwit2hero.com/excelformulas) you'll find a "Make me a millionaire" exercise that lets two details change: the rate of return, and the years you stay invested. The other details (the payment and the future value) stay the same for every calculation. The goal is to find different ways of reaching $1,000,000, without needing to make any regular payment.

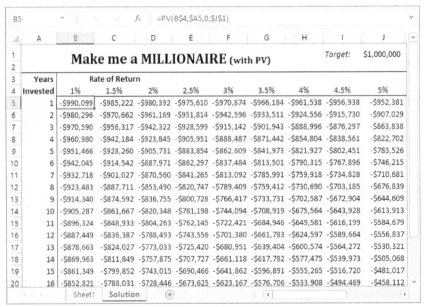

| B5 | | | f_x | =PV(B$4,$A5,0,$J$1) | | | | | | |

	A	B	C	D	E	F	G	H	I	J
1			**Make me a MILLIONAIRE** (with PV)						Target:	$1,000,000
2										
3	Years	Rate of Return								
4	Invested	1%	1.5%	2%	2.5%	3%	3.5%	4%	4.5%	5%
5	1	-$990,099	-$985,222	-$980,392	-$975,610	-$970,874	-$966,184	-$961,538	-$956,938	-$952,381
6	2	-$980,296	-$970,662	-$961,169	-$951,814	-$942,596	-$933,511	-$924,556	-$915,730	-$907,029
7	3	-$970,590	-$956,317	-$942,322	-$928,599	-$915,142	-$901,943	-$888,996	-$876,297	-$863,838
8	4	-$960,980	-$942,184	-$923,845	-$905,951	-$888,487	-$871,442	-$854,804	-$838,561	-$822,702
9	5	-$951,466	-$928,260	-$905,731	-$883,854	-$862,609	-$841,973	-$821,927	-$802,451	-$783,526
10	6	-$942,045	-$914,542	-$887,971	-$862,297	-$837,484	-$813,501	-$790,315	-$767,896	-$746,215
11	7	-$932,718	-$901,027	-$870,560	-$841,265	-$813,092	-$785,991	-$759,918	-$734,828	-$710,681
12	8	-$923,483	-$887,711	-$853,490	-$820,747	-$789,409	-$759,412	-$730,690	-$703,185	-$676,839
13	9	-$914,340	-$874,592	-$836,755	-$800,728	-$766,417	-$733,731	-$702,587	-$672,904	-$644,609
14	10	-$905,287	-$861,667	-$820,348	-$781,198	-$744,094	-$708,919	-$675,564	-$643,928	-$613,913
15	11	-$896,324	-$848,933	-$804,263	-$762,145	-$722,421	-$684,946	-$649,581	-$616,199	-$584,679
16	12	-$887,449	-$836,387	-$788,493	-$743,556	-$701,380	-$661,783	-$624,597	-$589,664	-$556,837
17	13	-$878,663	-$824,027	-$773,033	-$725,420	-$680,951	-$639,404	-$600,574	-$564,272	-$530,321
18	14	-$869,963	-$811,849	-$757,875	-$707,727	-$661,118	-$617,782	-$577,475	-$539,973	-$505,068
19	15	-$861,349	-$799,852	-$743,015	-$690,466	-$641,862	-$596,891	-$555,265	-$516,720	-$481,017
20	16	-$852,821	-$788,031	-$728,446	-$673,625	-$623,167	-$576,706	-$533,908	-$494,469	-$458,112

Sheet1 Solution ⊕

For example, look at cell B5 in this table. It tells you that if you are invested for only one year and your interest rate is a paltry 1%, you need to start with $990,099 to reach a million. But cell J18 tells a somewhat better story. Get 5% and stay invested for 14 years and you can start with just half the money, or $505,068.

You could make different types of tables to compare other approaches. For example, you could build a table that compares different interest rates and the effect of adding money in a monthly payment. To play with these scenarios, try out this exercise.

How much money can you borrow?

The PV can also calculate the future value of a loan. This is handy if you want to know, based on the current interest rate and your current monthly payments, how much money you can afford to borrow.

For example, say the bank charges 4.6% interest and you're able to pay $200 to your loan each month. If you want to pay the whole thing off in five years, how much can you withdraw today? The PV function has the answer:

```
=PV(4.6%/12, 5*12, -200, 0)
```

Notice the last parameter is 0, because you want your balance in the future to be $0— in other words, no more loan.

The formula answer is a positive $10,701.75, which is the money the bank can give you right now, in the present.

rate:	4.60%
# of years:	5
payment:	-$200.00
goal (fv)	$0.00
PV function:	$10,701.75

Of course, assumptions can trip you up. This calculation will change if the bank ratchets up the interest rate, so be warned. Try changing the interest rate in the formula above to 6%, for example, and see how much less you can afford to borrow with the same monthly repayment.

Finding the missing information

The FV function assumes you know everything about your investment except where it will end up. The PV function looks at things from the opposite side, and assumes you know everything about what you want from an investment except for the initial amount of money. The two formulas are a pair—they both look at an investment scenario and fill in the missing information.

But you can turn the same problem around to ask different questions. In fact, all the core financial functions are asking a variation of the same question. Each one finds the missing information in an investment calculation, assuming you know all the other details.

Every investment calculation has *five* key pieces of information: the present value, the future value, the rate, the regular payments you're making (if any), and the total time that you'll be invested (which is measured as a number of payment periods). When you ask a financial question, you provide all of these details except one. You then pick the Excel function that can give you the one piece of missing information.

The following table spells it out more clearly.

Present Value (starting value)	Future Value (ending value)	Rate (percentage it grows or shrinks)	Payment (amount of any regular contribution)	Number of Payments (the total time)	You Use This Function
Know	DON'T KNOW	Know	Know	Know	FV
DON'T KNOW	Know	Know	Know	Know	PV
Know	Know	Know	Know	DON'T KNOW	NPER
Know	Know	DON'T KNOW	Know	Know	RATE
Know	Know	Know	DON'T KNOW	Know	PMT

To use this table, find the row has "DON'T KNOW" for the piece information you're missing. For example, if you don't know the rate you need to achieve, skip down to the fourth row. Then, follow the row across to the right to get the name of the function that can calculate the missing detail. In this case, the RATE function can help you out.

You've already used the FV and PV functions. In the rest of this chapter, you'll see how you can answer three more financial questions with PMT, NPER, and RATE.

How many payments do you need to make?

Let's say you know the current value of your money and the final value you're trying to achieve, but you just want to know how long your financial journey will take. The function that figures this out is called NPER (for *number of payments*).

NPER takes these parameters:

```
NPER(rate, payment, pv, fv)
```

For example, let's say you've got $75 to put in an account each month, and that account pays 3.5% interest. You start with nothing, but you want to save up for the sweet $1,299 phone from Chapter 3.

Here's the formula that tells you how long it will take to meet your goal:

=NPER(3.5%/12, -75, 0, 1299)

The answer is 16.92. This means it takes 16 payments, plus one partial payment, to reach your goal. Payments in this example are per month, so this means it will take you 17 months to finish saving.

rate:	3.50%	
payment:	-$75.00	
start money (pv):	$0.00	
goal (fv):	$1,299.00	
NPER function:	16.921351	months
	1.4	years

You don't actually need to make monthly payments. You could just put some money in to start out and wait (and wait) for the magic of compound interest to get you to your goal. Here's an example that starts with you forking over $375:

=NPER(3.5%/12, 0, -375, 1299)

The news is not good. With no monthly contributions, your $375 won't grow to $1,299 until 426 periods have passed (that's roughly 36 years). So there's no need to line up outside the Apple store just yet.

As with all Excel's financial function, NPER works with loans just as easily as investments. Just set the present value to the amount you're borrowing and the future value to 0 to find out how long it takes to pay off your debt.

Here's an example with a $10,000 loan that you plan to pay off with $75 payments each month:

=NPER(5%/12, -75, 10000, 0)

Bad news: You won't be rid of the debt until you make 195 payments over 16 and a quarter years.

What rate do you need to earn?

If you find that the average Excel financial function is a bit of a downer, RATE might be more fun. It allows you to try some wish fulfillment—just tell Excel your investment goal, and it will conjure up a magical rate that will make it all work.

RATE takes these parameters:

```
RATE(number_of_periods, payment, pv, fv)
```

For example, if you want to double $5,000 in five years, with no extra payments, RATE can tell you how to make it a reality:

```
=RATE(5, 0, -5000, 10000)
```

The result of 14.87% tells you that you'll need quite an investment to meet your goal. Maybe it's time to scale down your plans.

# of years:	3
payment:	-$150.00
start money (pv):	$5,000.00
goal (fv):	$0.00
RATE function:	0.42% per month
	5.06% per year

RATE also works to tell you what interest rate you can afford on a loan. For example, if you want to pay off a $5,000 loan in three years, but you can only afford to pay $150 payments each month, this formula tells you the maximum annual rate you can manage:

```
=RATE(3*12, -150, 5000, 0) * 12
```

Notice that this RATE formula is assuming monthly compounding and monthly payments. To make that work, you need to multiply the years invested by 12 (as usual). You also need to multiply the result of the RATE function by 12 to turn the monthly interest rate into a yearly interest rate. The result, 5.06%, tells you that you can afford any loan that has that interest rate or less.

If you get a negative result from the RATE function, you've asked it an impossible question. For example, there's no way to pay $10,000 off with $25 payments per year, no matter what rate you get.

What payment do you need to make?

The last financial function, PMT, calculates the monthly payment you need to make your investment scenario work. It takes parameters in this order:

```
PMT(rate, number_of_periods, pv, fv)
```

Here's an example that asks how what payments you need to raise your $10,000 bank balance to $100,000 in 20 years, assuming you get 4% interest:

```
=PMT(4%/12, 12*20, -10000, 100000)
```

The result is -$212.05, meaning you need to pay that amount every month for 20 years to make your dreams come true.

rate:	4.00%
# of years:	20
start money (pv):	-$10,000.00
goal (fv):	$100,000.00
PMT function:	-$212.05

As usual, you can make a loan calculation by flipping the present value to a positive number (because this is money you get from the bank). Set the future value to 0 to calculate the payments you need to pay the loan off completely. Here's the formula that calculates the payment for an $10,000 loan at 8%, if you want to pay it off in six years:

```
=PMT(8%/12, 12*6, 10000, 0)
```

You're looking at $175.33 per month to get square.

The Last Word

In this chapter, you learned to use Excel's most important financial functions. You can think of these functions as a set of handy tools for all things to do with money. Using these tools, you can make future projections, long-term plans, and hard decisions, with no accountant required. And best of all, the advice Excel gives you is always free.

## Chapter 7

Manipulating Text

"You CAN'T ARGUE WITH ALL CAPS."

In your journey so far, you've learned to write formulas that work with numbers, dates, and times. But what if there was a way to take ordinary text and put *that* in a formula?

It's not as crazy as it seems. In fact, Excel has the tools to perform some text operations, like gluing bits of text together, taking them apart, replacing words, and changing capitalization. These are all specialized tricks—most of the time, you won't need to use them. But if someone hands you a workbook with sloppily scrambled text, these features will suddenly be a big help.

Manipulating Text—Why?

Just because you *can* do something doesn't mean you *should*. Before you learn about Excel's text-tweaking features, let's take a moment to see where they fit into the big picture.

Ordinarily, there's no reason to use a formula to change text. If you don't like the text you have on your worksheet, you can fix it with a quick edit. That's the easiest approach, after all.

But there are exceptions. For example, maybe you're using Excel to scrape details off of a website or pull information out of a *database* (a giant catalog of information, often stored on another computer). When you pull information out of another place, you're stuck with what you get. Maybe you want to put the customer's last name in an invoice, but you get the full name instead. Or maybe you want a properly capitalized city name for the address, but the database hands you one that's in UPPERCASE LETTERS. The solution is to transform the text you get into the text you want, using Excel formulas.

There's another reason you might end up with messy text. Maybe someone else sent you an ancient workbook of data with wonky formatting, and it's up to you to put this data into a clean, new Excel workbook. In this situation, you can use Excel's text features as a shortcut to fix up your text. The idea is to write a formula that makes the changes you need, then use that formula to change the text, and finally put the cleaned-up text in your new workbook. (When you're finished, you can get rid of the formulas.) This operation may sound like a complicated chore, but it's surprisingly useful. You'll try it out for yourself in Exercise #1.

But first, it's time to learn how Excel can change text.

Putting Text in a Formula

When you put text in a formula, you need to wrap it in quotation marks. (Technically, these bits of text are called *strings*.) The quotation marks prevent Excel from getting confused by spaces and special characters, or thinking that you're trying to use a strangely named function.

Here's an example of a formula with some text:

```
="Here's a bit of text"
```

The (rather unimpressive) result of this formula is the sentence "Here's a bit of text"

Excel lets you combine two pieces of text with an ampersand (&). Excel calls it the *concatenation* operator. (If you're having trouble finding it on your keyboard, you usually get it by pressing **Shift+7**.)

Here's a formula that gives you the same result as before:

```
="Here's " & "a bit of text"
```

Of course, there's no reason to type your text right into your formula. It's more likely that you want to combine the text in two cells, or combine the text in a cell with a bit of fixed text, like this:

```
="The cell in C3 has the content: " & C3
```

This takes part of a sentence and tacks the content from cell C3 on the end.

You can join as many pieces of text as you want. For example, if you have a first name in cell B2 and a last name in cell B3, you can join them together to make a full name, with a space in between, using this formula:

```
=B2 & " " & B3
```

You can use the & with cells that have numeric values. If you do, Excel grabs the full, unformatted number (no percent signs, commas, currency symbols, and so on) and turns that into text. If that's not what you want, Excel has a bunch of functions for turning numbers into specifically formatted text, including DOLLAR, FIXED, and TEXT.

Functions That Change Text

To do anything else with text you need the help of Excel's text functions. You can find the full list by clicking **Formulas** ▷ **Function Library** ▷ **Text**. The following sections take you on a tour of the most useful ones. At the end, you'll try an exercise that gets you to use the text functions for real.

Changing capitalization

Excel has three functions for dealing with uppercase and lowercase letters. LOWER changes all the uppercase letters in your text to lowercase letters. UPPER does the reverse—it changes lowercase letters to uppercase ones. But the most interesting capitalization function is PROPER, which makes the first letter in each word uppercase, and all the rest lowercase.

Here's an example:

=PROPER(B3)

Original Text	Result of PROPER
DOGS AND TIES	Dogs And Ties
bananas in pyjamas	Bananas In Pyjamas
There was a MAN. NO!	There Was A Man. No!

Trimming and cleaning text

Remember, Excel's text functions shine when dealing with second-rate text, like a list pulled out of a typo-filled spreadsheet from a decade ago. Excel even has a few functions that are dedicated to cleaning up sloppy text.

CLEAN is a straightforward function. Give it some text, and CLEAN removes non-printable characters from your text (weird symbols that aren't meant to be displayed). Why are there non-printable characters in your text? It's a surprisingly common problem that appears when you convert really old data.

TRIM works a similar magic. It cuts out extra spaces. So if your text has more than one space in a row, TRIM replaces it with just one space. And if you have extra spaces at the beginning or end of your text, TRIM chops them off. Why? Once again, because extra spaces are the curse of old data files.

Original Text	Result of TRIM
There are S P A C E S	There are S P A C E S
Hello	Hello
Here you are	Here you are

Replacing a piece of text

Excel has a neat SUBSTITUTE function that lets you do a search-and-replace inside your text. To use SUBSTITUTE you supply three parameters:

▶ The full text you're working with

▶ The text you're searching for (capitalization matters)

▶ The text you want to use as a replacement

Here's an example:

=SUBSTITUTE("Chocolate milk is a delight", "milk", "soy product")

The result of this switcheroo is this sentence:

Chocolate soy product is a delight

Here's an example that replaces three occurrences of the letter e with an empty piece of text (in other words, it removes the "e" and adds nothing in its place).

=SUBSTITUTE("This is a sentence without the letter e.", "e", "", 3)

The result is this:

This is a sntnc without th lttr .

Ordinarily, SUBSTITUTE replaces every occurrence of your search text. Optionally, you can add a fourth parameter to tell it which occurrence to replace. For example, if you use the number 2, Excel will replace the second match, but none of the others.

Getting a piece of text

Here's where things really heat up. Excel has a handful of functions that let you cut out small bits of text from a longer value. You can combine these with Excel's text searching functions to look for things inside your text and change them.

Warning: it's possible to do fairly sophisticated text processing in Excel, but the formula you need will be really ugly. That's because you'll need to nest one function inside another to perform the right sequence of searches, cuts, and joins. For simple modifications (like the one in the next exercise), it's no big deal. But more ambitious text-changing formulas can get so tangled that they aren't worth the struggle.

Now, meet Excel's text cutting functions: LEFT, RIGHT, and MID. The LEFT function cuts some text from the beginning of a text value. RIGHT grabs it from the end, and MID picks it out of the middle.

When using LEFT and RIGHT, you simply need to provide the text and tell Excel how many characters to cut. (Remember, a *character* includes letters, numbers, spaces, punctuation, and everything else that can go inside a piece of text.)

Here's an example that takes the first six characters from the text in cell A1:

=LEFT(A1, 6)

And here's an example that grabs the last six characters:

=RIGHT(A1, 6)

To use the MID function you need three parameters: the text, the position where you want to start cutting, and the number of characters you want to get. For example, if you want Excel to start at the fifth letter and take the next eight characters, you'd use this formula:

=MID(A1, 5, 8)

I'm sorry, Dave. I'm afraid I can't do that.

Result of =LEFT(C8, 9):   I'm sorry
Result of =RIGHT(C8, 16):   I can't do that.
Result of =MID(C13, 12, 4): Dave

The LEFT, RIGHT, and MID function only work if you know exactly where to go. They make sense if you have a strict format, like a product code where the first three letters always tell you the country where the product was made.

In other cases, you'll need to look in your text to find the position of some marker, and then use that position to decide where to cut. For example, maybe you're looking for a space or a comma so you can pick out an entire word. You'll use this approach in the exercise at the end of this chapter. But first, you need to meet two more functions that can help you count your way through the characters in a string of text.

Measuring the length of text

Excel's LEN function has a simple job. It looks at a piece of text and counts the number of characters, including spaces, punctuation, and anything else that's in there.

Here's an example:

```
=LEN(A1)
```

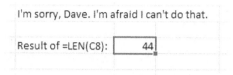

I'm sorry, Dave. I'm afraid I can't do that.

Result of =LEN(C8):   44

Knowing the length of some text isn't that useful on its own. But you can use this information with the text-snipping functions LEFT, RIGHT, and MID. For example, if you use this formula to get the first three characters out of some text:

```
=LEFT(A1, 3)
```

You can use this formula to get all the characters *except* the first three:

```
=RIGHT(A1, LEN(A1)-3)
```

This formula works because it gets the full length of the text and takes away three characters. It then grabs that many characters from the right-side. Result: you get everything but the beginning.

Searching text

The FIND function is another building block that you'll use when building more sophisticated text processing formulas. The FIND function looks at your text and searches for a character (or a bunch of characters in a row). Its result is a number that tells you the position of that text.

For example, if you write this formula:

```
=FIND("dog", "Hot dog")
```

The FIND function looks for the word "dog" in the text "Hot dog" and it gives you the answer 5. That's because the word "dog" starts in the fifth character position. If FIND can't find what you want, you'll get a #VALUE! error in your cell.

The FIND function also supports an optional third parameter that lets you tell it where to start the search. Consider this example:

```
=FIND("o", "Hot dog", 3)
```

The third parameter starts the search at position 3. So search skips right over the first "o" (in "Hot") and finds the second "o" at position 6 (in "dog").

The FIND search is case sensitive, which means if you search for "dog" Excel ignores "DOG". If you want to perform a search that isn't case sensitive, you can use the almost identical SEARCH function instead of FIND.

Exercise #1: Cleaning up a list of names

In this chapter you've seen a bunch of nifty functions for changing text. But you haven't seen a realistic example where someone needs to use them.

That's where this exercise fits in. Here's the situation. Your friend has just given you a workbook filled with a list of customer names. Sadly, the formatting of the names leaves a lot to be desired—everything is in full capitals and the first name and last name are crammed into a single column, which prevents you from sorting the people alphabetically by last name. But it's not your friend's fault. This list came from an old copy of and old spreadsheet that was converted from another file format by the company's office intern (a summer student who has long since moved on). Now you're left with the sloppy data.

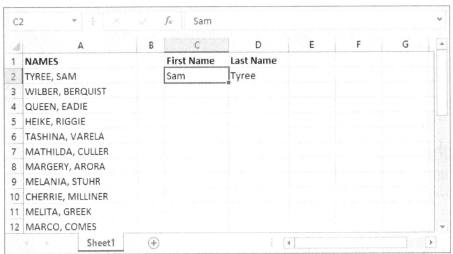

You *could* retype every single name by hand. But not only does this take a long time, it runs the risk of introducing typos and other mistakes. A better idea is to write a couple of Excel functions that can clean up the text. Through the magic of Excel formula copying, you can apply these formulas to the entire list. The last step is to convert the formula result to ordinary text. You can then remove the original data, leaving it nothing more than a bad memory.

The nicest thing about this example is that it gives you real insight into why Excel's text functions exist. To try it out, go to http://lab.halfwit2hero.com/excelformulas.

The Last Word

In this chapter, you took a detour down one of Excel's less trafficked alleyways. You learned how Excel lets you operate on text, using the concatenation operator (the &) and a whole family of functions.

By this point in the book, you've accumulated some serious function experience. You've tried out functions do everything from capitalizing a sentence to measuring triangle sides with trigonometry (see the "Princess of trig" in Chapter 4). It's time for a bit of a break.

In the next chapter, you won't pile on any new functions. Instead, you'll learn about Excel's naming feature, which lets you write clearer formulas and keep track of important cells.

Naming Cells and Ranges

"A rose by any other name would smell as sweet. Skunk cabbage, maybe not."

As you know, an Excel formula can grab any number from your worksheet by using a cell address. Once you get used to Excel's system of column letters and row numbers, cell references are easy to use.

Cell references tell Excel *where* to find a value, but that's about it. They don't tell you what's in that cell. They don't tell you why you need it. And they certainly don't warn you if you're pointing to the wrong cell.

That's where *named cells* come in handy. They let you use descriptive labels in your formula (like TaxRate instead of a cell reference like E2). In this chapter, you'll learn how to name cells and ranges. You'll also take a quick detour to see Excel's table feature and learn how it uses names.

Cleaner, Neater Formulas

By this point, you've seen dozens of formulas in action. It doesn't scare you to see a pile of cell references. When you stare down a formula like this:

=B6*B7

You know exactly what it does, mathematically speaking. (You're multiplying two numbers together, of course!) But it's not as easy to figure out *why* you're multiplying these two numbers together.

Now consider this formula:

=ListPrice*TaxRate

Although this formula has the same effect, you can immediately see that its calculating the amount of tax on a purchase. You might even recognize that this is the calculation from the "Buy a phone" example in Chapter 3.

You can make a similar change to this formula:

=B6+B8

So that it explains itself, like this:

=ListPrice+Tax

Now you're not just adding two numbers. You're calculating the cost of a new phone.

How to name a cell

Once you've decided that you want to name a cell, it's easy. Start by moving to the cell you want to name. Then, look at the Name Box, which appears in the top-left corner just above your worksheet.

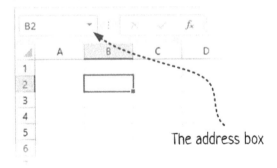

The address box

Ordinarily, the Name Box shows the address of your current cell. In the example shown here, that's cell B1.

Chapter 8: Naming Cells and Ranges

But the Name Box doubles as a cell naming tool. Just click inside it, type the name you want to use, and press **Enter**. This process is called *defining* a name.

Cell names can use letters and numbers, but no spaces. If you want to make a cell name that fuses together more than one word, you can distinguish the words with capitalization (for example, TaxRate) or underscores (Tax_Rate). You can't use a name that looks like a cell reference (like B10), not even for an April Fool's Day prank.

Excel remembers which cells have names. If you move to an ordinary (unnamed) cell, the cell address appears in the Name Box. But if you move back to your named cell, the name appears in the Name Box instead of the cell address.

The Name Box has one quirk: it does double-duty as a tool that lets you jump around your worksheet. If you type a cell address in the Name Box and press **Enter**, Excel takes you to that cell. The same thing happens if you type a name that you've already used—Excel brings you to the corresponding cell when you press **Enter**. This can be a bit of shock if you're trying to name a cell and you don't realize you're using a name you've already defined.

Using a name in a formula

Once you've defined a name, you can use it in a formula in the same way that you use an ordinary cell reference. In fact, Excel will even help you out with its handy autocomplete feature. Once you type the first letter of the name in your formula, Excel pops up a list of names and functions that match.

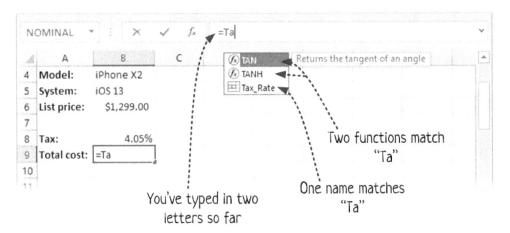

You've typed in two letters so far

Two functions match "Ta"

One name matches "Ta"

The functions show up first in the list, with a tiny picture of "fx" in a circle next to each one. (No, the fx does not stand for special effects. In function talk, the fx is short for F(x), which means "a function that operates on whatever data you give it.")

The names show up after the functions. There's a tiny picture of a worksheet next to each name.

If you want to take advantage of this shortcut, keep typing until the name you want is at the top of the list, or press the down arrow key to move down the list until your name is highlighted. Then, press **Tab** to insert the name into your formula.

There's one other way to quickly pop one of your names into a formula. While you're writing the formula, you can pick your name out of the **Use in Formula** list. Just click **Formulas** ▷ **Defined Names** ▷ **Use in Formula** to pop up a full list with all the names in your workbook, and click the name you want to use.

Making Excel put names in a formula

Ordinarily, it's up to you to use your names in a formula. But Excel has an interesting feature that can scan the formulas you've already written and replace ordinary cell references (like B7) with the corresponding names you've defined (like TaxRate). This trick is called *applying names*.

Here's how to do it:

1. If you want to apply names to a single cell, move to that cell now. If you want to apply names to a bunch of cells at once, select all the cells. (If you want to select the whole worksheet, here's a shortcut: click the top corner of the worksheet grid, immediately to the left of the A column.)

Click here to select
EVERYTHING

2. Look at the **Formulas ▷ Defined Names ▷ Define Name** button. On the right side of this button is a small down-pointing triangle. Click it to show a menu, and then choose Apply Names.

3. In the Apply Names window, you choose the names that Excel will use when it works its substitution magic. To pick a name, click it so it becomes highlighted in blue. (To unpick a name, click it a second time.) There's no harm in picking all your names, which means Excel will replace all the references it finds that match any one of your names.

4. Click **OK**. Excel scans all the selected cells, checks each reference in each formula, and replaces any references that match one of the names you picked.

Applying names isn't much of a convenience if you're just trying to change a single formula. But if you've recently added names to a worksheet with dozens of formulas, it's a handy shortcut to update your formulas without risking a mistake. You'll get to try this feature yourself in the next exercise.

It's worth pointing out that Excel has another automatic feature that works with names. You can ask Excel to scan a selection, look at your captions or column headings, and create names for your cells automatically. This feature may sound neat, but in practice it's a disaster. You'll end up with a jumble of names you don't want, most of which will be awkwardly long. If you want to take a look for yourself, direct your attention to the **Formulas** ▷ **Defined Names** ▷ **Create From Selection** button. But don't say I didn't warn you.

Exercise #1: Adding (and using) names

Now that you've learned how to create names, it's time to try a quick exercise that lets you put your new skills into practice.

Head to http://lab.halfwit2hero.com/excelformulas and open the "Adding names" workbook. It brings back the "Buy a new phone" workbook from Chapter 3. But now you're going to name the important cells. Then, you'll revise the formulas to use the names instead of boring old cell references. It shouldn't take long at all!

Browsing your names

Here's a nifty way to see all your names, and skip around the worksheet to find them. In the Name Box, click the down-pointing triangle (on the right side). This drops open a list of all the names you've created in this workbook, ordered alphabetically. Click one of these names to jump over to that cell.

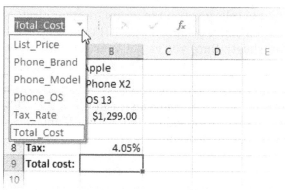

Sometimes, you might see a named cell being used in a formula, but you won't remember what cell it points to on your worksheet. In this situation, the Name Box list gives you a quick way to match a name to its cell.

When you give a cell a name, it's bound to be longer than an ordinary cell address. You might find that some names don't fit in the Name Box, forcing Excel to chop off the end when it displays them. Don't worry—you can make the Name Box big enough to show even the longest names. The secret is knowing where to drag.

In between the Name Box and the Formula Bar is a tiny vertical line of three dots. You'll know you're in the right place when your mouse pointer changes to a left-right arrow. Click here, and pull to the side. Drag it to the right to make the Name Box bigger (and the formula bar smaller, because space don't come for free).

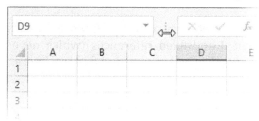

Naming a range

So far you've been naming individual cells. But Excel also lets you name a whole group of cells. This is handy if you're using functions that use ranges, like SUM, AVERAGE, MAX, and MIN. For example, you can practice naming ranges with the "Take the temperature" exercise from Chapter 4.

To name a range, begin by selecting all the cells you want to group together. Grab as many as you want—you can even select an entire column or more (by clicking on the column headers at the top of the worksheet). Once you've got your selection right, carry on as usual: type the name in the Name Box and press **Enter**.

When you name a range, the name doesn't show up in the Name Box when you're on just one of the cells in that range. For example, if you name a select of cells B3 to B8, you won't see the name appear when you're positioned on cell B7. But if you select exactly the same range, the name will appear in the Name Box again.

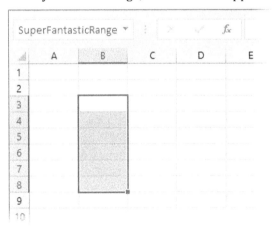

Names are fixed references

In Chapter 3 you learned about the difference between relative references (which shift around when you make formula copies) and fixed references (which never change). But here's something you might not realize: *every name is a fixed reference.*

Say you have a formula that uses names, like this:

```
=B3*TaxRate
```

If you make a copy one row down, you'll end up with this:

```
=B4*TaxRate
```

In the copy, Excel changed the relative reference B3 to B4, but it didn't touch the TaxRate name. Is this what you want? It all depends. In some situations, a fixed reference keeps Excel from moving a reference to the wrong place. In other situations, fixed references prevent you from using Excel's copy-and-adjust feature to quickly fill up a column of formulas. And sometimes you don't plan to make any formula copies, so it doesn't matter what kind of references you have.

But this behavior does mean that certain types of references are more suited to be named cells. For example, if you're using exactly the same value in a bunch of formulas, it makes sense to name that cell. But if you're using a cell in a table row, a name may be less useful.

Consider the third exercise from Chapter 3:

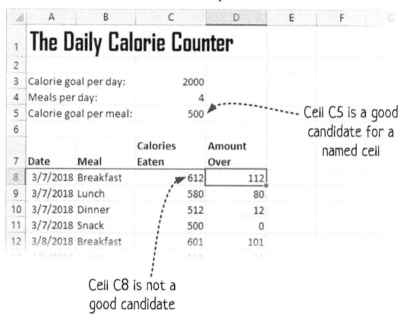

The formulas, which calculate your excess calorie consumption, are in column D. Cell C5 (the calorie goal) is used in every formula, so it's a great choice for a named cell. But the cells that record the calories eaten in each meal (cells C8, C9, C10, and so on), aren't as good candidates for naming. That's because each formula uses a different cell. You'd need to name each cell in the table, using awkward names like CaloriesEaten1, CaloriesEaten2, and so on. And you wouldn't be able to copy use Excel's copy-and-adjust feature to fill in all the formulas in a single step.

It will take a while before you get a true sense of when using names can help you and when it's just a headache. But the more you know about how names work, the better decisions you can make.

A quick refresher: Should you use names?

It's time for some real talk. As you've seen, using named cells is easy. You could put this book down right now start packing your worksheet with dozens of names. But should you?

Not necessarily. There are plenty of good reasons to use names, but also some reasons to avoid them. Here are the most obvious advantages:

▶ They make what a formula does clearer.

▶ They can help you catch formula mistakes. (For example, the formula =TaxRate*NumberOfPurchases doesn't sound like it makes sense.)

▶ They show up in handy autocomplete lists when you're writing your formula.

▶ They let you jump straight to important cells (through the list in the Name Box).

However, names are not necessarily a path to Excel paradise. There are also some drawbacks you need to consider:

▶ It takes more time to add all your names, and more effort to make sure you're choosing good ones.

▶ You might be forced to make long names that just clutter up your formulas, like AverageTemperatureFirst60DaysOfJuly.

▶ When you look at a formula that uses names, you can't tell where it's getting its data from at a glance. (Instead, you might need to track mysterious names down with the Name Box, or edit the formula so that Excel highlights the cells it uses.)

▶ Cell names are fixed references. This can limit your ability to copy and reuse formulas.

So what's the best advice for using cell names? First, remember that a handful of names is pretty easy to work with. But piles of names can become difficult to manage. One good strategy is to use names for your most important cells. Good candidates are cells that are used in many formulas and have an obvious meaning. Bad candidates are cells in tables and cells that are used just once.

The Name Manager

What if you make a name and then decide you don't need it anymore? Or you create a name but you end up moving your data to a different place? The Name Box lets you create names, but it doesn't give you a way to change names or delete them.

That's where the Name Manager comes in. It's a handy tool that lets you see all the names you've created and change them. To use the Name Manager, choose **Formulas** ▷ **Defined Names** ▷ **Name Manager**.

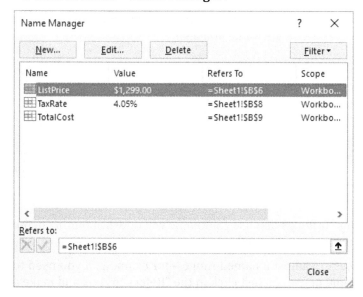

The Name Manager window lists the names in your workbook, shows the current value in each named cell, and shows the corresponding cell references.

The Name Manager is a nice place to look at your names. But if that's all you could do there it wouldn't be much different than the Name Box. But it turns out that the Name Manager doesn't just let you look at your names—it also lets you *change* them.

Pointing a name to a different cell

Maybe you've rearranged your worksheet and you've moved the tax rate to a different cell. Using the Name Manager, you can point your old TaxRate name to the new cell, and everything will be right once more. Here's how:

1. Click the name you want to change in the Name Manager.

2. Click in the "Refers to" box. Be careful here. You don't want to click inside the name. You want to click to the right, so the text cursor appears at the end of the reference.

3. Now find the new cell you want to use on your worksheet. You might need to drag the Name Manager window to the side to see the cell you want underneath.

4. Click the cell. The new address will appear in the "Refers to" box. (If your text cursor is in the wrong spot, Excel might go wonky and start putting a formula in

the "Refers to" box. If this happens to you, just delete everything in the "Refers to" box and then click the worksheet cell you want.)

5. Click the tiny checkmark on the left side of the "Refers to" box to make your change permanent. (If you forget to take this step, Excel will ask if you want to save your change when you close the Name Manager.)

Once you make a change, any formulas that use your name will now be pointing to the new, proper cell. There's no need to edit anything.

You can use the same process to adjust a named range—for example, if you need to make it bigger to take in some new data. Just click in the "Refers to" box and make a new selection on your worksheet, with as many cells as you need.

Renaming a name

You can also use the name manager to change one of your names. For example, maybe you decide that the cell you named TaxRate should really be SalesTaxPercentage. To make this change, follow these steps:

1. Click the name you want to change in the Name Manager.

2. Click the **Edit** button. A new window, called Edit Name, will appear.

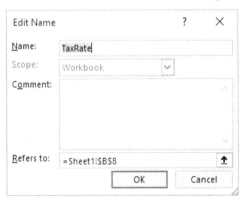

3. Type the new name in the Name box. You can also add comments help you remember what the name is for, but don't bother. (That feature is for Excel savants when they create weird formula name hacks and other name witchcraft.)

4. When you've finished making your changes, click **OK** to put your change into effect.

If you rename your name, Excel does you the courtesy of updating the name everywhere in your worksheet, meaning your formulas will keep working. So if you change TaxRate to SalesTaxPercentage, any formula that uses TaxRate is seamlessly updated to use SalesTaxPercentage instead. Nice!

Deleting a name

The Name Manager also helps you out if you want to delete a name. To do that, click the name in the list and then click the **Delete** button.

But be warned that Excel won't fix up any formulas that use the deleted name. Instead, any formula that attempts to use a deleted name will fail and show a #NAME? error on the worksheet. It's up to you to find and correct those formulas.

Using the same name in different worksheets

If you look closely at the cell references in the Name Manager, you'll notice that every reference is a fixed reference and every reference includes the worksheet name. So instead of seeing a cell address like B8, you'll see something like Sheet1!$B$8.

You might remember this naming technique from Chapter 3. It lets you refer to a cell on one worksheet (like Sheet1) from another worksheet (say, Sheet2). This system means that when you create a name, you can refer to it on any worksheet, anywhere in your workbook. Technically, Excel says your name has *workbook scope*.

This naming system has a side effect: you can't define the same name on more than one worksheet. For example, if you name a cell SalesTotal on one worksheet, you can't name another cell SalesTotal on a different worksheet. This can be a problem if you want to put a bunch of similar worksheets into a workbook. (For example, imagine you're creating a workbook that shows company sales in different months, and you have worksheets named January, February, March, and so on.)

To avoid this problem, you can create names with *worksheet scope*. You can then use the same names on different worksheets. Here's how:

1. Click the name you want to change.

2. Click the **New** button. The New Name window will appear, which basically the same as the Edit Name you saw before.

---

3. Fill in the Name box (with the name, naturally) and the "Refers to" box (with the cell address, by clicking the cell you want to name).

4. Change the Scope setting from Workbook (the standard choice) to the worksheet where you want to use your name. This is almost always the worksheet with the named cell. So if you're creating a SalesTotal name for a cell on Sheet1, you should pick Sheet1.

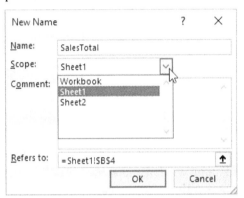

5. Click **OK** to create the name.

If you create a name that's scoped to Sheet1, you can use that name in any formula that's in any cell in Sheet1. You can still refer to the cell from another worksheet if you want, but you'll need to include the worksheet name, just as you would when referring to an ordinary cell. For example, the reference Sheet1!SalesTotal tells Excel to look on Sheet1 for a cell named SalesTotal. You can use this reference on any worksheet in your workbook.

To see an example of names with worksheet scope, check out the Solution worksheet in the first exercise (earlier in this chapter). The Solution worksheet uses worksheet scope so that its names don't collide with the names you're going to add to Sheet1.

Crazy name tricks: don't do it

When you create a name in the Name Manager (as you just did), you can pull off some more exotic naming tricks. For example, you can create a name that doesn't actually point to a cell, but uses a fixed value, like 413. (You just type this value in the "Refers to" box.) Or, you can create a name that is actually a *formula* that uses a combination of cells, operators, and functions. You can even create names that use relative references instead of fixed references, which means the address shifts around—an extremely confusing situation considering that you don't actually see the cell reference in your formula, only the name.

These tricks are impressive, but they really aren't worth the headaches. It's better to use safe names that behave the way everyone expects. This reduces the risk of making a mistake or confusing yourself in the future.

Names in Tables

There's one other place that you can find named cells—when you use Excel's table feature. The difference is that you don't create table names. Instead, you create the table and Excel supplies the names.

Before you go any further, let's get one thing straight. Plenty of worksheets have information that's arranged like a table, with its data in rows and columns. (You've seen more than a few examples in the exercises for this book.) But Excel's *table feature* enhances ordinary tables. It adds fancy frills like sorting and quick formatting.

If you've never used an Excel table before, the next section will fill you in on the basics. But if you already know how to create an Excel table, you can skip ahead to the "Table names" section to see how tables use names.

Try it out: Create a table

Here's how tables work:

1. You select some cells that have information arranged in tabular form. (In other words, the data is arranged in regular rows and columns.)

2. You officially tell Excel "Hey, this is a table here!"

3. Excel changes the way your table cells look and adds some extra features to make your life easier.

The best way to understand how tables work is to create one of your own. You can try this out with any worksheet that has a few rows of information. If you don't have anything suitable, open up the "Calorie counter" example from Chapter 3.

To identify your table to Excel, move to one of the cells in the table (any one will do) and choose **Insert** ▷ **Tables** ▷ **Table**.

Excel looks at your worksheet and selects all the cell that are part of your table, including the column headings. Then it pops up the Create Tables window to tell you what it found.

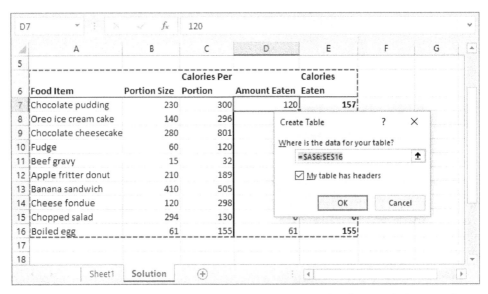

In the Calorie counter, Excel gets all the cells from A6 (at the top-left corner) to E16 (at the bottom-right).

If something is wrong here—for example, you don't want all the columns in your table—you can change the selection now. Otherwise, click **OK** to tell Excel to go ahead and create the table.

When you create a table, your cells change. The most obvious change is *banding*, which is the way Excel shades alternate rows so you can easily tell one row from another.

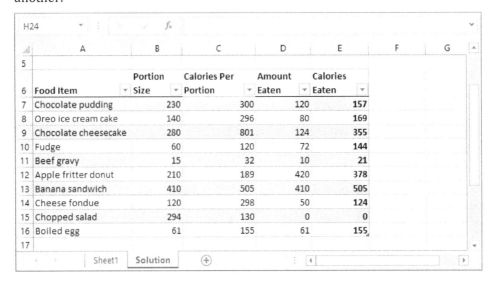

You'll also see a drop-down button at the top of each column. (Click it to pop open a menu with a pile of nifty sorting and filtering commands.)

You can always change your table back to ordinary cells. Just click inside your table and pick **Design** ▷ **Tools** ▷ **Convert to Range**. But really, why would you?

Some essential table features

We won't spend too much time exploring tables. But if you're completely new to them, here's a quick rundown of a few of their most useful features:

▶ **Formatting.** When you click inside a table, Excel adds an extra **Design** tab to the ribbon. The **Design** tab has plenty of options for formatting a table, but the fastest are *quick styles*, which let you apply a coordinated set of borders and shading. You can choose from a gallery of options in the **Design** ▷ **Table Styles** section of the ribbon.

▶ **Automatic growing.** You don't need to keep adjusting a table to make it bigger. Just type a new row at the bottom, and the table automatically expands to swallow the new data.

▶ **Quick sorting.** You can sort a table by any column, alphabetically, numerically, or by date. Just click the drop-down button in one of columns to pop up menu with plenty of choices. For example, if you click it in a column of numbers, you'll see the choices **Sort Smallest to Largest** and **Sort Largest to Smallest**. Don't be afraid to experiment, because you can change your sort as often as you want.

▶ **Filtering.** You can temporarily hide the rows you don't want to see. This is a great way to focus on a small section of data when you have a huge table of information. Once again, the choices are in the column menu. For example, in a column of numbers you'll see a **Number Filters** option that lets you set an upper or lower limit (so you only see values over 100, or values under 1000).

You'll get to practice the formatting, sorting, and filtering features with a real live table in the upcoming exercise, "Your wedding budget."

Table names

Here's something you might not know about tables: they take your column headings and use them to create named cells.

For example, consider the calorie counter example that you just saw converted to a table. Right now, cell E7 has a "calories eaten" formula that looks like this:

=D7/B7*C7

You can rewrite this to use the column names. The easiest way is to use Excel's point-and-click formula feature, which you first met in Chapter 3. The idea is to click the cells you want as you write the formula, which gets Excel to fill in the correct name. That way, you avoid typos.

To recreate the formula shown above with column names, start by typing the equal sign and then click cell D7. Then, press the / for division, and click cell B7. Finally, type a * for multiplication and click cell C7. Excel will create a formula that looks like this:

`=[@[Amount Eaten]]/[@[Calories Per Portion]]*[@[Portion Size]]`

At first glance, this formula looks intimidating. Because the column names include spaces, Excel needs to wrap them in square parentheses. It also adds the @ symbol to indicate that you want the value from the current row for this column. So the name `[@[Amount Eaten]]` is equivalent to an ordinary reference to cell D7.

The problem with column names is that Excel always use the caption at the top of the column. If you have a long column heading, like "Portion Size (grams)," you'll get an even uglier column name, like `[@[Portion Size (grams)]]`.

To avoid extremely awkward column names, you may want to change the text in your column heading to something simpler. Don't worry if you've already used the old name, because Excel automatically adjusts your formulas to the new name when you edit the column. Unfortunately, there's no way to make the automatic column name different from the text in your column heading.

You can also use the column names to refer to the range of *all* the cells in a column. For example, let's say you want to calculate the average of all the calories eaten. You could use a formula like this:

`=AVERAGE(Table1[Calories Eaten])`

The only unusual part of this formula is the name Table1. Excel gives every new table an unhelpful name like this. To choose a better name, click a cell inside your table. Then, go to the **Design** ▷ **Table** section of the ribbon. You'll see a box with the table name "Table1." Change it to something else, and Excel will update your formula to match.

The nice thing about column names is that they grow or shrink with your table. So if you add a row to the table, it's automatically added to the column range. That means it's included in your average calculation, without you needing to lift a finger.

It's hard to get comfortable with table names without trying them for yourself. In the next exercise you'll get to write several formulas that use table names.

Exercise #2: Your wedding budget

The best way to get understand table names is to use them yourself. In this exercise (available on the tutorial site http://lab.halfwit2hero.com/excelformulas), you start with a list of wedding expenses. Your first job is to transform these ordinary cells into a genuine table that looks like this:

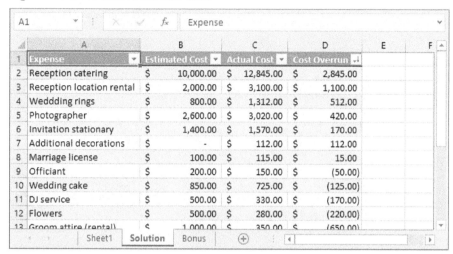

Once you've created your table, you'll get to work with it. You'll use column names inside the table and outside it. You'll also try out a few of Excel's table features, like sorting and filtering.

If you're at all uncertain about how tables work, this exercise is essential practice.

The Last Word

In this chapter, you took a thorough look at cell names, which let you stick descriptive labels on individual cells or on entire ranges. Cell names can make cryptic formulas more readable, and they can help you keep track of important cells.

It's worth pointing out that whether you use names or not, it won't change what your formulas can do. Instead it's all part of the "art" of writing Excel formulas. Now that you're becoming a seasoned formula writer, you're going to spend less time thinking about how to get an answer, and more time thinking about the best way to design your sheets and organize your cells.

Setting Conditions

"If you love Excel with no conditions, you will like it even better with them."

An ordinary formula does what you tell it to do. You throw some numbers, operators, and functions together, and the formula goes to work to give you the answer. But what if your formula could make a decision?

In this chapter you'll learn to write *conditional formulas*—formulas that can go one way or another, depending on a condition that you set. For example, you can use this technique to stop a formula from hitting an error if your numbers aren't right. Or, you can use it to create a formula that changes its calculation to suit different data. All you need to unlock these superpowers is to understand conditional logic.

Introducing Conditional Logic

Before you can write a conditional formula, you need to know what a condition is.

A *condition* is a snippet of logic that can be either *true* or *false* (but not anything in between). Here's an example of a condition:

```
5 = 3
```

If you translate this condition to human language, it says "5 is equal to 3." This condition is very obviously false, because 5 does not ever equal 3.

A condition doesn't need to stick to hard numbers. You can also use cell references, like this:

```
A1 = 3
```

This condition says "the number in cell A1 is equal to 3." This may be true or it may be false. It depends what number is in cell A1.

The logical operators

Every condition revolves around a *logical operator*. You just saw the simplest logical operator, the equal sign. Condition also use the greater than (>) and less than (<) signs to compare numbers, like this:

```
A1 < 3
```

This condition is *true* if cell A1 has a number that is less than 3 (examples include 1, 2.35, or -15940). It's also true if cell A1 is blank. However, this condition is *false* if A1 has a bigger number (like 3 or 934786), or if cell A1 has some text in it.

You can combine the equal sign with a greater than or less than sign to make the "less than or equal to" operator (that's <=) and the "greater than or equal to operator" (that's >=). Here's an example:

```
A1 <= 3
```

The equal sign always comes after the less than or greater than sign. In this example, the condition is true if cell A1 holds the number 3 or a number that's less than 3.

You can make one last operator by combining the less than and greater than signs, like this:

```
A1 <> 3
```

This is the "not equal to" operator. It's true if cell A1 has anything other than the number 3. Possibilities include other numbers, text, or a blank value. But if cell A1 actually does hold a 3, the condition is false. In other words, the "not equal to" operator is the exact opposite of the equal sign.

Try it out: Writing a condition in a formula

Conditions are a basic ingredient that you use to with other functions. For example, you can use conditions with the IF functions to build a formula that makes a decision.

You'll get to that in a moment. But first, you should stretch your conditional logic muscles by writing a few conditions of your own. Here's how:

1. First, fire up Excel with a new worksheet.

2. Move to cell A1, and type the number 12. (We're using 12 for an example, but there's nothing special about it.)

3. Move to the cell underneath (that's cell A2), and type the number 6.

4. Move down one more cell (to A3). This is where you're going to write your condition.

5. Type the equal sign (=) to start your formula.

6. Now you can type in a condition. For this example, you'll use the condition A1=A2. Here's the complete formula you'll end up with:

=A1=A2

This may seem strange to you, because it looks like a formula with two equal signs. Just remember that the two equal signs are doing completely different things. The first equal sign starts the formula, and the second equal sign is part of the condition.

7. When you finish the formula and press **Enter**, Excel evaluates your condition. In this case, 12 does not equal 6, so the condition A1=A2 is false. Excel displays the word FALSE in the cell in all uppercase letters.

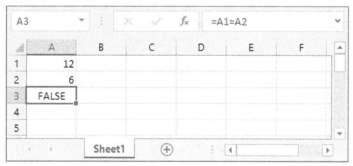

Now you can experiment by changing the values in A1 and A2. For example, change A2 to 12 and the condition becomes true. You'll see a capital TRUE appear in cell A3 to alert you to this fact.

You can also tinker with the formula to try different conditions. Before you go any further, try these variations:

```
=A1<A2
=A1>A2
=A1<>A2
```

You can also put calculations in a condition. Consider this formula:

```
=A2/A1=2
```

To understand what's happening here, remind yourself to ignore the first equal sign, which is only there to tell Excel you're writing a formula. The rest of condition asks a straightforward question: if you divide A2 by A1, will you get 2? In other words, is A2 exactly twice as big as A1? Change the values of A2 and A1 to make this true.

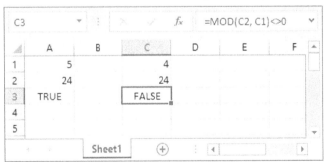

You can also use a function in your condition. Here's an example:

```
=MOD(A2, A1)<>0
```

To understand a condition with a function, think through the formula step by step. Excel will evaluate all the functions and perform all the calculations before it evaluates your condition. In this example, Excel starts by using the MOD function, which gets the remainder left over after dividing two numbers. If A2 divides evenly by A1, the result of the MOD function is 0, and the result of this condition is false. If there's remainder left over after the division, MOD gives some number other than 0, and the condition becomes true. Try it out in your worksheet.

Remember, this is just practice. There's no practical reason to put a condition in a worksheet cell. However, you'll use exactly the same type of conditions with Excel's conditional functions. You'll get started in the next section.

How a Formula Makes a Choice

Several Excel functions use conditions. The most flexible of them all is the IF function, which lets you switch between two different values or formulas.

Here's the outline of the IF function:

```
IF(condition, use_this_if_true, use_this_if_false)
```

The first parameter is a condition. The IF function evaluates this condition. If it's true, the IF function carries on with the second parameter. If the condition is false, the IF function switches to the third parameter.

To see how this works, imagine a very simple example:

```
=IF(A1<A2, 100, 200)
```

Excel begins by evaluating the condition A1<A2. If it's true (A1 really is less than A2), Excel uses the second parameter, which means it shows the number 100 in the cell. If the condition is false, Excel uses the third parameter and shows the number 200 instead.

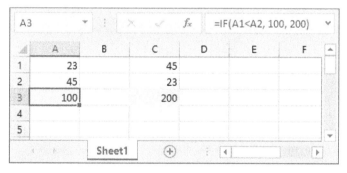

Basically, the IF function works like the ordinary conditions you typed directly into in the worksheet. But instead of showing TRUE or FALSE, the IF function chooses between the two values you've given it.

Making useful conditional formulas

Right now, the IF function doesn't seem terribly useful. But there plenty of creative ways you can use it to save work in a formula.

For example, imagine you're running one of those poncy restaurants that automatically slaps a 15% surcharge on people in large groups (because it doesn't trust them to tip nicely). Here's an Excel formula that puts this rude rule into effect:

```
=IF(B2>7, C2*115%, C2)
```

B2 holds the number of diners, and C2 holds the dinner charge. If the number of diners tops 7, the extra rate kicks in. This example uses multiplication, but there's no limit to what you can stuff into your true and false parameters. You're free to use mathematical operators, brackets, and nested functions.

It only seems fair to add another formula that explains when the surcharge has been added. In this case, you're going to need quotation marks, because you want your IF function to show one of two text values. (Without the quotation marks, Excel assumes you're trying to create an expression with numbers, names, or functions.)

```
=IF(B2>7, "15% surcharge added for large group", "")
```

In this cell, a text message appears if you've got a large group. Otherwise, the last parameter comes into effect, which uses " " to designate empty text (nothing at all!).

B4				f_x	=IF(B2>7, "15% surcharge for large group", "")		
	A	B	C	D	E	F	G
1	Table tab:	$942.23					
2	Number of guests:	12					
3							
4		15% surcharge for large group					
5							
6							
7							

Sheet1 (+)

You can use the IF function to create all kinds of conditional formulas. For example, you could create a formula that applies a handling fee of 5% to an order, but cap it so you never charge more than $25. If you assume the total cost is in a cell named OrderTotal, here's a formula that calculates the handling fee:

```
=IF(OrderTotal*5%>25, 25, OrderTotal*5%)
```

In other words, if 5% of the order total is more than 25, use the number 25, otherwise use 5% of the order total. If you want to get even fancier, why not round your handling fee to the nearest penny:

```
=IF(OrderTotal*5%>25, 25, ROUND(OrderTotal*5%, 2))
```

You'll get to practice writing some conditional formulas like this in the upcoming exercise. But first you need to learn to combine more than one condition at a time.

Combining conditions

Sometimes, you might what to make a decision that requires more than one condition. For example, maybe you only want the 15% surcharge to kick in if the group is large (more than 7 people) *and* the bill is large (at least $300).

To apply these conditions, you can use the helpful AND function. It takes two parameters (you put one condition in each parameter), and then provides a final answer of true or false. If both conditions are true, then AND is true also. But if either one of the conditions is false, AND is false.

Here's an AND condition that fuses together the two restaurant conditions:

```
=AND(B2>7, C2>=300)
```

Type this in a cell and you'll see the word TRUE or FALSE appear on your worksheet. That's not particularly helpful. What you really want to do is slip the AND function into the IF function you used earlier, so it can make a more nuanced decision about when to slap on the surcharge. Here's how:

```
=IF(AND(B2>7, C2>=300), C2*115%, C2)
```

Now the surcharge calculation (C2*115%) kicks in when both conditions are true.

Excel has a similar OR function. Like AND, the OR function takes two conditions. But unlike AND, the OR function is true as long as *at least* one of its conditions is true. So this formula is true if you have a large group or they have a big bill, but you don't need both to be true at once:

```
=OR(B2>7, C2>=300)
```

And lastly, there's a NOT function that reverses your logic. For example, consider this IF statement, which asks if the table has more than 7 people:

```
=IF(B2>7, "15% surcharge added for large group", "")
```

It's equivalent to this formula with NOT, which asks if the table does *not* have 7 people or less:

```
=IF(NOT(B2<=7), "15% surcharge added for large group", "")
```

You never need to use NOT, but sometimes it allows you to write your conditions in a way that seems clearer or just makes more sense to you.

Adding more outcomes

When you use the IF function, you get to choose between exactly two outcomes. But sometimes you need more possibilities. You might want to swap between three, four, or more different calculations.

For example, let's say you've invented an extraordinarily rude restaurant that ratchets up the automatic surcharge as you add more guests. The 15% surcharge applies for tables with more than 7 guests (just like it did before). But now there's a new rule. If the table has more than 12 people, you up the 15% surcharge to a gouging 20%. You can apply this adjustable surcharge with IF through the magic of *nested functions*.

Let's walk through the solution. You start with your first test, which asks "are there more than 7 people at the table?" If not, your calculation is easy—stick with original total. Here's the in progress formula (with the missing information represented by a question mark):

```
=IF(B2>7, ?, C2)
```

But what if there are more than 7 people? Well, now it's time to use a second IF function to test if you have more than 12 people. The trick is that you slip this second IF function right inside the first one, like so:

```
=IF(B2>7, IF(B2>12, C2*120%, C2*115%), C2)
```

Confused? Let's break this down. If the first IF function finds that there are more than 7 people, it uses the second parameter, which has another IF function. This second IF function checks if there are more than 12 people. If there are, the second IF function adds the 20% surcharge. If there aren't, the second IF function sticks with the 15% surcharge (because it already knows there are more than 7).

The basic idea is that you are giving Excel a series of IF tests. When one of them is true (or false), another IF function asks a new question. It can be difficult to keep track of which path Excel follows through a formula with nested IF functions, so be careful! You may want to watch Excel work through your formula one step at a time with the Evaluate Formula window, which you learned to use in Chapter 5 (see the section "Try it out: Watching Excel calculate a date").

You can keep sticking one IF function inside another until your formula is impossibly complicated. For example, here's an extension to the previous formula that slaps on an extra $75 flat fee for tables that have more than 20 people:

```
=IF(B2>7, IF(B2>12, IF(B2>20, C2*120%+75, C2*120%), C2*115%), C2)
```

In this example, there are three nested IF functions. Technically, Excel lets you nest formulas up to 64 levels deep. That's a lot of decisions!

Exercise #1: The school of Excel

It can be difficult to puzzle out a formula that uses one or more IF functions. You'll understand it better if you take the time to build your own conditional formulas.

That's the task you'll undertake in this exercise, "The school of Excel" (get it at http://lab.halfwit2hero.com/excelformulas). You begin with a worksheet of student marks, calculated based on two tests and a final exam. You'll use conditional formulas to choose between different grading options. And you'll use nested IF functions to show the letter grade that matches each student's final percentage score.

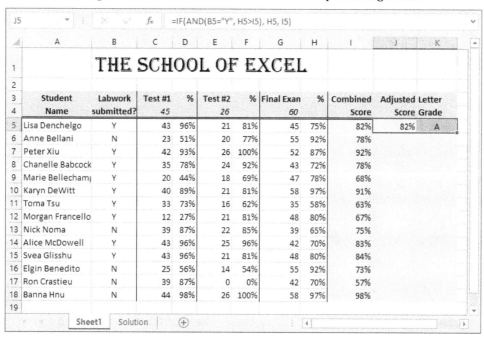

This is a pretty substantial tutorial. You'll get to practice your formula inspection skills, you'll used fixed references to control formula copying, and you'll engage in some fairly sophisticated conditional logic. By the time you've worked your way to the end, you'll have seen several conditions at work.

Conditions with dates

In all the examples you've seen so far, you've been using conditions to check *numbers*. For example, you've been asking if one number is less than, more than, or equal to another number.

Conditions with numbers are the most common types of conditions. But you can also use conditions that examine dates or even text. With dates, all the same logical operators apply, including the greater than and less than symbols. For example, if you want to ask if a certain date is before today, you could use this function:

```
=IF(B2<TODAY(), "The project is overdue!", "")
```

This formula displays a warning message in the cell if the date in cell B2 falls before the current date. This type of comparison makes sense, because dates are actually numbers (as you'll remember from Chapter 5). So it's no challenge to compare two

---

date numbers and find out which one is smaller than the other (and therefore earlier than the other, according to the calendar).

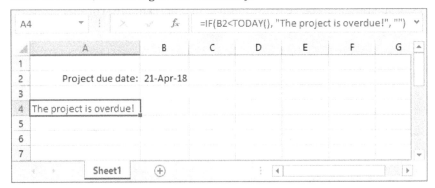

When comparing dates, it's often useful to use different date functions. For example, you can use the familiar YEAR, MONTH, and DAY functions to get part of a date and use that in your condition. This formula checks if a date falls in July or August:

`=IF(OR(MONTH(B2)=7, MONTH(B2)=8), "Summer break!", "")`

Because this formula is looking for dates in either month, you need to use the OR function to yoke the two conditions together.

This formula doesn't do much—it just displays a "Summer break" message if the date is in July or August. In a more realistic example, you might add extra time to a project due date to compensate for the good weather.

The only limit to conditional date formulas is your imagination. If you use the other date functions from Chapter 5, you'll have no trouble writing conditions that check for workdays, days of the week, and the end of the month.

Conditions with text

Text values have their own oddball rules. When you compare text values, Excel doesn't pay attention to capitalization. Consider this formula:

`=IF(B2="VOID", "This value is void.", "")`

It displays a message if cell B2 contains the word VOID, void, vOiD, and so on.

If you want to match a text value exactly, you need the help of the **EXACT** function. It gives a true result if text values match with exactly the same capitalization:

`=IF(EXACT(B2, "VOID"), "This value is void.", "")`

But the weirdest way to use text conditions is with the greater than or less than symbols. They perform an *alphabetical* comparison, so one text value is considered "less" than another if it comes before it in dictionary order. That means "apple" is less than "banana" but not "aardvark". This type of comparison isn't terribly common, but Excel makes it possible.

The Is Functions

Excel has a small group of "Is" functions that give you information about other cells. For example, you can check whether a cell holds a number, or if a formula in another cell causes an error.

The "Is" functions are natural partners for the IF function. The pattern goes like this: you find out something with an "Is" function, and you decide what to do about it with the IF function.

One example is the ISBLANK function, which looks at a cell and checks whether it's empty. Here's how you use ISBLANK to check cell A3:

```
=ISBLANK(A3)
```

If you put this formula in a cell, you'll see the word TRUE or FALSE appear, depending on what's in cell A3.

You won't use the "Is" functions on their own. Instead, you'll combine them with the familiar IF function to make a conditional formula. For example, here's a formula that checks if a number in a cell is even using the ISEVEN function and uses the IF function to decide what to do about it. If the number is even, it divides it by 2. But if the number is odd, this formula adds 1 (to make it even) and *then* divides by 2.

```
=IF(ISEVEN(C3), C3/2, (C3+1)/2)
```

If you want to browse through the list of "Is" functions, you can find them all in the **Formulas** ▷ **Function Library** ▷ **More Functions** ▷ **Information** list in the ribbon. You'll find functions for checking if a cell contains text, numbers, formulas, and more.

Here's an outline of the most useful "Is" functions:

Function	It's true if...
ISBLANK	The cell is empty
ISNUMBER	The cell has a number. (Dates and time values count too.)
ISTEXT	The cell has some text.
ISFORMULA	The cell has a formula in it.
ISERROR	The cell has a formula in it that causes an error. (It will be showing an error code like #NAME?)
ISNA	The cell has the #N/A error (not available), which indicates a failed lookup, using the functions you'll see in Chapter 10.
ISERR	The cell has an error in it. However, the #N/A error doesn't count (unlike with the ISERROR function).
ISEVEN	The cell has an even number.
ISODD	The cell has an odd number.

Checking for an error

The ISERROR function is a particularly handy tool. You can use it to avoid having an error show up in your worksheet.

At this point, you might wonder "Avoid an error? Why don't I just fix my formula?" And it's true that there are no excuses for leaving formula mistakes in your worksheets. But sometimes a formula encounters an error not because you've done something wrong, but because some of the data you have is missing or doesn't apply to the type of calculation you're attempting to perform.

For example, imagine you've got a job mowing lawns in the summer. You plan to keep track of how much money you make and how many hours you work. You calculate your earnings per hour with a formula like this:

=Earnings/Hours

This formula is nice and readable because it uses cell names, which you learned about in Chapter 8.

However, there's a problem. When you create the worksheet, you haven't yet made any money or worked any hours. As a result, your formula shows the infamous #DIV/0! (divide by zero) error, which makes your worksheet look broken.

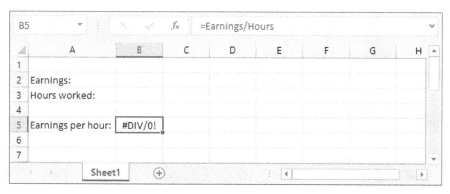

You can sidestep this problem by checking if it's safe to perform your division before you attempt it. To do this, you ask the ISERROR function to check if the division would cause an error. If it does, you show something else, like a text message or a blank value. If ISERROR doesn't encounter an error, you can safely carry on with the calculation.

Here's a formula that uses this safeguard:

```
=IF(ISERROR(Earnings/Hours), "", Earnings/Hours)
```

Now if there's nothing filled out in the Hours cell, your calculation shows a blank result.

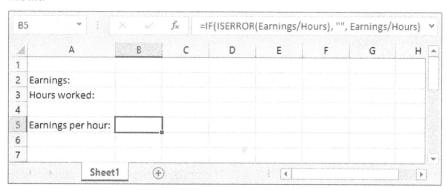

This might seem like extra work just to avoid an error message for an incomplete worksheet. But imagine a more sophisticated example where you perform a bunch of different calculations and divisions, some of which may not apply. For example, you might create a worksheet for your lawn care company that includes formulas for different types of work (lawn mowing, hedge trimming, flower planting, weeding, and so on). Every time you work on someone's lawn you fill out a copy of this spreadsheet with the work you did. (So if you didn't do any weeding, you leave that section blank.) In this situation, you don't want a pile of error messages showing up for calculations that don't apply.

Testing for an error is such a common technique that Excel even has a shortcut for it. You can use the IFERROR function, which combines the IF function and the ISERROR function. The idea with IFERROR is that you supply the error-causing calculation only once, followed by the fallback value Excel should use in the case of a problem.

Here's a compact formula that uses IFERROR to duplicate the previous example:

```
=IFERROR(Earnings/HoursWorked, "")
```

If there's no error, Excel knows that you want to show the result of the calculation, so you don't need to repeat that information in your formula. If there is an error, Excel shows the second parameter (in this case, it's a blank value).

Excel has a similar IFNA function that tests specifically (and exclusively) for the #N/A error. You'll use this when you're writing lookups, as you'll see in Chapter 10.

Conditional Calculations with Ranges

When it comes to making decisions, the IF function is the superstar. But IF isn't the only function that uses conditions.

Excel also has a set of conditional functions that work with *groups* of cells. All of these functions work the same way—they use a condition to decide what cells to include when performing a calculation. For example, you might use SUMIF, a conditional SUM function, to add up attendance records from a certain date, or expenses from a specific store. Or you could use AVERAGEIF to calculate the average test mark of the youngest students.

Excel has several conditional functions that work with ranges, and they all behave the same. You'll start by taking COUNTIF for a spin.

Conditional counting

In Chapter 4 you met the COUNT function, which counts a range of cells. Now you're ready to see it's grown up cousin, COUNTIF, which only counts the cells that meet a condition you set.

The COUNTIF function takes two parameters. The first parameter is the range of cells you're counting, just like you use with COUNT. The second parameter is a piece of text that has part of a condition. You'll understand it best if you see an example.

Here's a formula that counts all the values greater than 10:

```
=COUNTIF(B3:B20, ">10")
```

The weird part here is the condition, which doesn't quite match what you've seen before. That's because the COUNTIF function actually needs to evaluate a slightly different condition for each cell it looks at. For example, in this case COUNTIF starts by checking cell B3 and asking if B3>10. Then it looks at cell B4 and tests if B4>10. And so on.

Because the COUNTIF needs to make a different condition for each cell, you don't supply the whole condition, like you do with the IF function. Instead, you give COUNTIF a snippet of text that it uses to build its *own* conditions. When you make this snippet of text, you leave out the first value (the cell that you're checking), and you start with one of the logical operators, like the equal sign, greater than sign, or less than sign.

Using multiple conditions

COUNTIF demands that cells meet a single condition, but you can enforce more with COUNTIFS (note the "s" at the end of the function name). You just repeat the range and add a second condition. For example, this formula counts cells that have a value above 10 but less than or equal to 20:

```
=COUNTIFS(B2:B20, ">10", B2:B20, "<=20")
```

You can add as many conditions as you one. (OK, not really, but Excel allows exactly 255 criteria, which is way more than you should try to stuff into one formula anyway.) Each time you add a condition, you also need to specify the cell range.

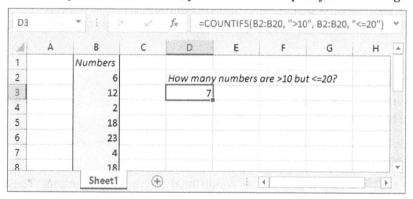

You might wonder why you need to repeat the cell range over and over again in your formula. That's because you might use different conditions on different ranges. This sounds odd, but it makes perfect sense when your data is arranged in a table. In this case, you can use different conditions to check different columns. If all the columns pass their conditions, COUNTIFS counts that row.

Here's an example that checks two columns and then decides whether to count a row in table. In order to be counted, the number in column B must be greater than 10 and the number in column C but be more than 25:

```
=COUNTIFS(B2:B20, ">10", C2:C20, ">25")
```

And here's this formula at work, where it counts the number of people who are older than 10 and who owe more than $25 to the library:

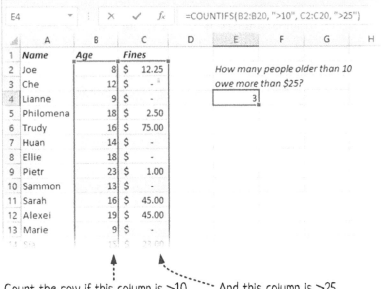

Count the row if this column is >10 ···· And this column is >25

You'll write fancy formulas like this to count students in the exercise at the end of this chapter. But first it's time to check out the other conditional formulas that work with cell ranges.

The family of conditional functions

So far you've seen two conditional functions that work with cell ranges: COUNTIF and COUNTIFS. Excel has several other helpful choices:

▶ SUMIF and SUMIFS perform conditional sums. They only add the cells that meet your conditions.

▶ AVERAGEIF and AVERAGEIFS perform conditional average calculations. They only take into account the cells that meet your conditions.

▶ MAXIFS and MINIFS look for the highest or lowest value in a range. But, as you probably already expect, they only pay attention to cells that meet your conditions.

There are two ways to use these functions. The simplest way is to use one range for each condition. Check out this formula, which adds the numbers in a range that are less than 100:

```
=SUMIF(B2:B20, "<100")
```

Chapter 9: Setting Conditions

So if cell B2 is greater than 100, Excel adds that to the total, then it checks cell B3, and so on, until it checks cell B20 at the end of the range.

The other possibility is to use one range for each condition, and *another* range for your calculation. Here's an example that uses column B to decide what rows to include, but adds the information that's in column C to calculate the sum:

```
=SUMIF(B2:B20, ">10", C2:C20)
```

In this example, if the cell B2 has a number that's greater than 10, Excel adds the value from C2 to the sum. If B3 meets the condition, Excel adds C3, and so on, until it's finished working itself through the whole range.

This technique only works if your information is arranged in a proper table. You'll try it out for yourself in the student exercise in the next section.

	A	B	C	D	E	F	G	H
	NOMINAL		fx	=SUMIF(B2:B20, ">10", C2:C20)				
1	Name	Age	Fines					
2	Joe	8	$ 12.25		Total fines of people			
3	Che	12	$ -		older than 10			
4	Lianne	9	$ -		$ 191.50			
5	Philomena	18	$ 2.50					
6	Trudy	16	$ 75.00					
7	Huan	14	$ -					
8	Ellie	18	$ -					
9	Pietr	23	$ 1.00					
10	Sammon	13	$ -					
11	Sarah	16	$ 45.00					
12	Alexei	19	$ 45.00					
13	Marie	9	$ -					
14	Sia	15	$ 23.00					

Sheet1

Exercise #2: The school of Excel (part 2)

Is this final exercise you'll return to the list of student marks you worked with before. But instead of making conditional calculations for each student, now you'll use the conditional functions that work with ranges, like COUNTIF and AVERAGEIF. With the help of these functions, you'll answer some questions about the overall distribution of marks. For example, how many students received As or Bs? What was the average score of an A student? And did the students who didn't submit their labwork do worse than those who did?

To get these answers, head to http://lab.halfwit2hero.com/excelformulas and try it yourself.

The Last Word

In this chapter, you looked at how you can use conditions to cram a bunch of choices into a single formula. Excel gurus can construct conditional formulas that are almost mini-programs, with logic that navigates through layers of possibilities. If you use Excel long enough, you'll find plenty of situations where you can get yourself out of a sticky situation with the right use of the IF function.

You're now nearing the end of your Excel exploration. You have just one more type of function to consider. In the next chapter, you'll use lookup functions to search through tables and extract important bits of information.

Using Lookups

"There is always a way to go if you look for it."

Lookups are one of Excel's best magic tricks. They get a formula to search a table of information and pull out the data you want. For example, you can use a lookup to scan a list of people and get the age of a specific person. Or, you can use a lookup to search a product catalog and get the price of a specific item.

Lookups are particularly useful for building smart spreadsheets that can help *automate* business tasks. That's a fancy way of saying that you can use Excel to take a tedious spreadsheet job—one that you need to do all the time—and make it happen more quickly and with less work.

For example, let's say you need to go through a class list and generate reports. You can use lookups to extract the information for a student and put it into the outline of a report. (Just rinse and repeat for each student in the class.) Or, say you want to create an invoice for a new order. Using lookups you can fetch the information from a product table, saving you the trouble of typing in all the prices. In this chapter, you'll see these types of examples in action.

How to Search a Table

At its simplest, a lookup is just a way to hunt through a table and pull out an important bit of information.

In the ribbon, the **Formulas** ▷ **Function Library** ▷ **Lookup & Reference** list holds the lookup functions. This list also has a bunch of oddball functions that don't fit into any of the other categories, including functions that convert formulas to text, swap rows with columns, and shift cell references around. Along with these quirky functions are the two powerhouses of lookups: VLOOKUP and HLOOKUP.

The V and the H stand for *vertical* and *horizontal*, which is the direction the lookup works. For example, with a vertical lookup you search vertically down a table. Once Excel finds the match, it can grab another value from a different column in the same row.

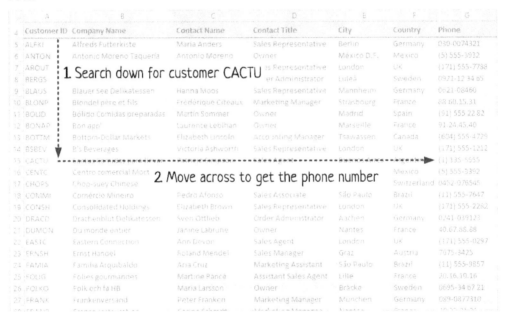

A horizontal lookup scans horizontally across a range of cells. Once it finds a match, you can get another value from a different row in the same column.

1. Search across for "Clown fish"

	A			E	F	G
1	Cow	Grizzly bear	Clown fish	Chilean flamingo	Blue whale	Horse
2 Phylum	Chordata	Chordata	Chordata	Chordata	Chordata	Chordata
3 Class	Mammalia	Mammalia	Actinopterigii	Aves	Mammalia	Mammalia
4 Order	Artiodactyla	Carnivora	Perciformes	Ciconiiformes	Cetacea	Perissodactyla
5 Family	Bovidae	Ursidae	Pomacentridaie	Phoenicopteridae	Balaenopteridae	Equidae
6 Genus	Bos	Ursus	Amphiprion	Phoenicopterus	Balaenoptera	Equus
7 Species	taurus	arctos horribilis	ocellaris	chilenis	musculus	caballus

2. Move down
to get the species

Either way, the principle is the same. You hunt down a piece of information you *know*, and slide over to a related piece of information that you *need*.

Now that you understand what lookups do, you're ready to craft one of your own.

The anatomy of a lookup

It's time to check out **VLOOKUP**, the meaty Excel function that does the work when you need to perform a vertical lookup. Here's an outline of **VLOOKUP** and its parameters:

```
VLOOKUP(lookup_value, table_range, column_index, range_lookup)
```

VLOOKUP needs four parameters of information. They include:

▶ **lookup_value**. This is the value you're searching for. For example, maybe you're looking for a product named "Magic Toaster" or the person with the ID number 40023.

▶ **table_range**. This is a range that holds the table you're using. It doesn't actually need to include the whole thing, but it does need to start with the column where you're performing your lookup and it needs to include the column with the information you want to retrieve.

▶ **column_index**. This tells Excel how to move from your lookup column to the column that has the information you want. (More on that in a moment.)

▶ **range_lookup**. This tells Excel whether you want to insist on an exact match or find the closest value. Usually, you'll set this to **FALSE** to insist on exact matches, but you'll also learn how to use range lookups later in this chapter.

None of these parameters is particularly complicated. But, as you'll see, there are a few tricks to getting them to work right.

Choosing a good lookup value

To perform a successful lookup, you need to carefully choose your lookup value (that's the value you're using to find the row you want). The first rule is that your lookup must use a column with *unique values.* That's because the VLOOKUP function stops when it finds the first match, and you don't want to risk settling on the wrong row. For example, you shouldn't perform a lookup based on a customer's last name, because more than one person may have the same last name. Instead, use a piece of information that's guaranteed to be unique. Possibilities include social security numbers or driver's license numbers, assuming you have this information for everybody in your list.

Here's the first part of a VLOOKUP formula, with the lookup value (a social security number) filled in:

```
=VLOOKUP("529-80-3271", ...
```

The best kind of information to use for a lookup is some sort of made-up ID value. For example, a small business might assign a unique number to each new customer (like 3001, 3002, 3003, and so on). Or, if a business is keeping track of invoices, it might assign a special code to each one, like "MRYBL12-001." (In this example, the first part of the billing code represents an abbreviated version of the purchasing company, and the second part is a sequence number that starts at 001 and goes up with each new purchase.) Lookups ignore capitalization, so it doesn't matter whether you type MRYBL12-001 or mrybl12-001. They're the same in Excel's eyes.

Of course, the right lookup value depends on what's in your data. If you're dealing with a large list of information (or pulling information from a database), you probably already have some type of unique identifier to use.

Getting the right range

The next step is to figure out the range to use for your lookup. Take a closer look at the following list of customers.

	A	B	C	D	E	F	G
4	Customer ID	Company Name	Contact Name	Contact Title	City	Country	Phone
5	ALFKI	Alfreds Futterkiste	Maria Anders	Sales Representative	Berlin	Germany	030-0074321
6	ANTON	Antonio Moreno Taqueria	Antonio Moreno	Owner	México D.F.	Mexico	(5) 555-3932
7	AROUT	Around the Horn	Thomas Hardy	Sales Representative	London	UK	(171) 555-7788
8	BERGS	Berglunds snabbköp	Christina Berglund	Order Administrator	Luleå	Sweden	0921-12 34 65
9	BLAUS	Blauer See Delikatessen	Hanna Moos	Sales Representative	Mannheim	Germany	0621-08460
10	BLONP	Blondel père et fils	Frédérique Citeaux	Marketing Manager	Strasbourg	France	88.60.15.31
11	BOLID	Bólido Comidas preparadas	Martín Sommer	Owner	Madrid	Spain	(91) 555 22 82
12	BONAP	Bon app'	Laurence Lebihan	Owner	Marseille	France	91.24.45.40
13	BOTTM	Bottom-Dollar Markets	Elizabeth Lincoln	Accounting Manager	Tsawassen	Canada	(604) 555-4729
14	BSBEV	B's Beverages	Victoria Ashworth	Sales Representative	London	UK	(171) 555-1212
15	CACTU	Cactus Comidas para llevar	Patricio Simpson	Sales Agent	Buenos Aires	Argentina	(1) 135-5555

The lookup column   The column with the information you want

In this example, the unique values are special customer codes, like "ALFKI" and "BERGS," which show up in column A. The goal is to get a specific customer using their customer code, and then grab the corresponding phone number, which is in column G. The table spans the rows 5 to 93, so the range you need is A5:G93.

Here's the first part of the lookup formula you need:

```
=VLOOKUP("BSBEV", A5:G93, ...
```

If you wanted to look up the customer's contact title (from column C) or city (from column E), you could shrink the range down to include fewer cells (A5:C93 stops at the contact information, A5:E93 stops at the city information). But it's probably easier to use the whole table, with all its columns. There's no harm in including extra columns. Often you'll want to write several lookup formulas that retrieve different pieces of information from the same table, and you may as well use the same range for all of them.

The third parameter is a number tells Excel how to get from the lookup column to the column that has the information you want. The number is an index, with 1 representing the first column in the range, 2 representing the second column, and so on. In the customer list example, you use 7 because G is the seventh column in the range A5:G93.

```
=VLOOKUP("BSBEV", A5:G93, 7, ...
```

You can now finish off the formula by supplying FALSE for the last parameter, which tells VLOOKUP you need an exact match:

```
=VLOOKUP("BSBEV", A5:G93, 7, FALSE)
```

The result of this lookup is the text (171) 555-1212, which is the phone number for the customer BBSEV.

There's one unbreakable rule for the range you use with VLOOKUP. The column you're using for the lookup must always be the *first* column in the range. You'll find that most tables are already arranged this way. But if your table has the lookup column on the other side, you'll either need to do some rearranging or you'll need to rely on the MATCH and INDEX functions described later in this chapter.

Lookup forms

Instead of sticking your lookup value right in your formula, it often makes sense to put in a cell. That way, you can quickly look up different information.

Here's a revised formula that grabs the customer code from cell C1:

```
=VLOOKUP(C1, A5:G93, 7, FALSE)
```

Using this formula, you're able to build a basic *lookup form*—a handy tool for searching for bits of information you need. I—in this case, the phone number of any customer you want to call.

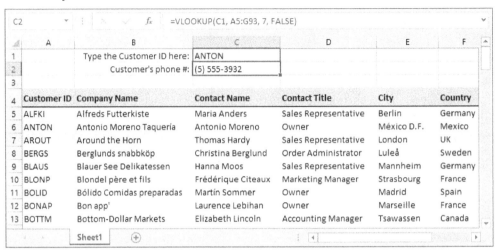

Using this strategy, you can build even fancier forms. The central idea is that you provide one detail (a unique ID) and your lookup formulas automatically fill a bunch of other cells to match. Here's an example that creates a customer mailing address for any customer you specify:

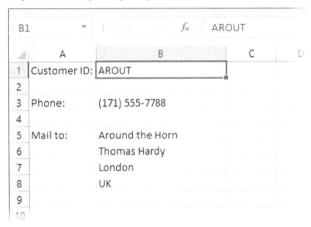

There are five lookup formulas in this example, in cells B3, B5, B6, B7, and B8.

Creating this example is easy. You just need to make more lookups, one for each piece of information. You can use the same range in every formula, just change the column index to get the information you want. And to make things really neat and tidy, you can put the table with the data in one worksheet and your form in a *different* worksheet. That makes sense, because you don't want to clutter your customer mailing form with a huge list of all your customers.

You'll try this technique out for yourself in the catering company exercise. But first, you need to consider one more topic: dealing with lookup failures.

Dealing (gracefully) with failed lookups

Lookups don't always work. Obvious mistakes (like trying to use an index number for a column that isn't in your range) will cause the formula to fail with a #REF! or #VALUE! error. If this happens to you, review the formula and make it right.

A trickier problem is if Excel can't find the lookup value. This doesn't mean your formula has a mistake. It simply means the row you want isn't in the list. When that happens, you'll get an #N/A ("not available") error.

For example, consider what happens if you attempt to find non-existent customer TACO in the customer list:

In situations like these, you don't necessarily need to fix anything. The #N/A error code is just Excel's way of telling you that the lookup value doesn't exist. However, error codes can scare people, and if someone sees a bunch #N/A messages popping up in a spreadsheet, they might just assume something is broken. A more serious problem occurs if you need to perform other calculations with your cells, like sums and averages. In this situation, an #N/A error in one cell is enough to break your calculation.

A friendlier way to deal with lookups that don't find anything is to use the IFNA function. It works exactly like the IFERROR function you used in Chapter 9. You give IFNA two parameters: the expression you want to use, and a fallback value it should show if the expression fails with an #N/A error.

Here's an example that shows a "not found" message when a lookup fails:

```
=IFNA(VLOOKUP(B1, Sheet1!A5:G93, 7, FALSE), "[NOT FOUND]")
```

If your lookup hits a different error, the IFNA function doesn't intervene, and you'll still see that error code appear in your cell.

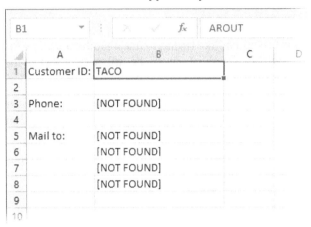

The IFNA function is also a good idea if your lookup form starts out blank. For example, in the customer lookup form you might leave cell B1 empty, because you don't know which customer you're going to use. However, the lookup functions don't hold back on blank values. When cell B1 is blank, your lookup formulas will attempt to find a blank value in the lookup column. And because there's no blank customer, you'll get an #N/A error. To avoid getting #N/A errors for blank values, use IFNA to substitute something else (or just the blank text "").

Exercise #1: Look Up! Catering

It's one thing to learn how to write a lookup formula. It's another step to understand what makes lookup formulas so useful—and how you can use them to quickly fill in complicated spreadsheets, saving you oodles of work.

Fortunately, there's an exercise that can help you get a handle on the practical side of lookup formulas. You start with a lengthy price list for a catering company. Using this price list and a handful of lookup formulas, you can create an order form that grabs all the pricing information automatically.

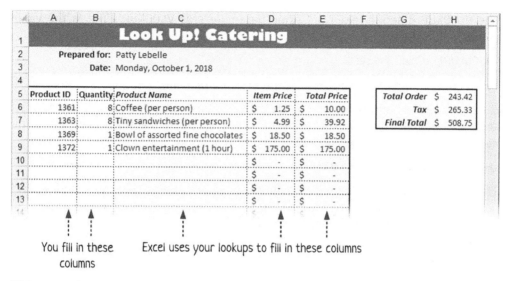

You fill in these columns

Excel uses your lookups to fill in these columns

This example is an excellent introduction to *real-world* spreadsheet building (in other words, building the sort of spreadsheets that business rely on in real life). Check it out on the tutorial site at http://lab.halfwit2hero.com/excelformulas.

Looking the other way

All the examples you've seen have used VLOOKUP, which is the most common of Excel's lookup functions. However, VLOOKUP has a sister HLOOKUP function that does horizontal lookups. It works exactly like VLOOKUP, but it works with tables that are arranged the other way around.

The following example presents a table of animal information. You can get the details on several species, including cows, bears, clown fish, flamingos, and more.

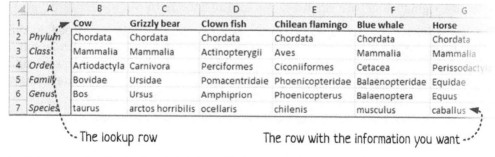

The lookup row

The row with the information you want

In this example, the lookup's job is to find some information about the animal of your choice. For example, you might decide you want to know more about whales. Using HLOOKUP, you find the "Blue whale" column, and then you skip down the column until you get to what you want.

The HLOOKUP function takes the same parameters as VLOOKUP. First is the value you're looking for:

`=HLOOKUP("blue whale", ...`

Remember, it doesn't matter if your capitalization matches.

Next you need to identify the range that holds the table. Your lookup row needs to sit at the top of your range. In this example, the range **B1:G7** captures everything you need.

`=HLOOKUP("blue whale", B1:G7, ...`

The third parameter is no longer the column index—it's now a *row* index. It tells Excel how many rows to count down to find the information you want. In this example, you need to count down to the seventh row, which has the species information, so you use a value of 7:

`=HLOOKUP("blue whale", B1:G7, 7, ...`

And finally, add the FALSE parameter to tell Excel you want an exact match, just as you did with VLOOKUP:

`=HLOOKUP("blue whale", B1:G7, 7, FALSE)`

Now the formula is complete. The result is the blue whale species name, "musculus," from cell F7.

Super Advanced Lookups

Every Excel guru knows a few lookup tricks. Some are only useful in specific, rare situations. Others are ridiculously complicated to understand. But every once in a while, the right lookup trick can make you into an Excel hero.

The best advice is not to memorize every exotic lookup technique. Instead, in the following sections you'll learn a few ways to extend ordinary lookups. Understand these, and you'll be able to unravel a more complicated lookup formula in someone else's spreadsheet. And if you face a lookup challenge of your own, you'll know enough to track down a solution on the web and adapt it for your needs.

How to find matches that aren't exact

The lookups you've used so far have insisted on exact matches. If you're looking for a customer with an ID of 243, that's exactly what you'll find. And if there's no such customer, you'll face the infamous #N/A error.

If you're searching for a specific row in a table, exact lookups make the most sense. But sometimes you're dealing with a looser set of data, and you want to find the closest match. Check out the following table, which has a list of temperatures recorded on some days in July.

◢	A	B	C	D	E
1	*New York Daily Temperatures*				
2	July	High (°F)			
3	1	79			
4	2	90			
5	4	84			
6	6	77			
7	7	81			
8	9	83			
9	10	82			
10	13	93			
11	14	70			
12	17	84			

This example has a list of temperature readings, but some days are missing. If you ask VLOOKUP what the temperature is on the eight day in July, it has two choices—it could tell you #N/A (there is no such day reading) or 81 degrees (here's a reading from the day before, which is the best you can do). The second answer is what VLOOKUP calls a *range lookup*, and it's what you get if you switch the final parameter from FALSE to TRUE.

Here's the formula that gets the temperature using a range lookup:

```
=VLOOKUP(F3, A3:B22, 2, TRUE)
```

You could leave out the final parameter altogether. It's optional, and if you don't include it, VLOOKUP (or HLOOKUP) assumes you want TRUE.

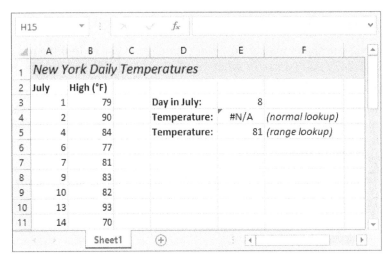

Range lookups only work if you're table is sorted by the lookup column. That's because VLOOKUP travels through the lookup column looking for a match. As soon as it finds a value that's bigger than what you want, it gives up, and returns the value before it (the one that's too small). So if you're looking for July 8, when you reach July 10 the VLOOKUP function throws in the towel and takes the preceding date, July 7, instead.

If your table isn't sorted, Excel will think it's pickling the closest match, but it'll give you something else, or fail altogether with an #N/A error. So don't even bother trying.

Range lookups are particularly useful if you're dealing with a constantly increasing value in your lookup column. For example, if you've got a column that records the total amount of money you've spent, a range lookup can find the moment just before you go over budget.

How to find matches using two columns

In a perfect world, every time you perform a lookup you'll search for a unique value in a single column. But sometimes you might get a table that isn't so ideal. For example, maybe you have a list of people with first names and last names but no unique ID values or codes. What should you do?

One solution is to create a combined field that *is* unique. For example, maybe you are reasonably certain that there's no one in your list with exactly the same combination of first and last name. You can take advantage of this fact by creating an extra column that fuses together the two names. For example, if you have first names in column B and last names in column C, you might put a formula like this into the corresponding cells in column A:

=B4 & " " & C4

Chapter 10: Using Lookups

This is a formula that pastes together text, like the kind you saw in Chapter 7. It joins the first name, followed by a space, followed by the last name, and puts the combined result in the cell.

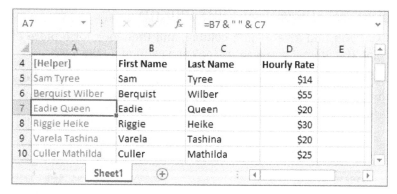

A combined column like this is called a *helper column*, because it only exists to help your lookout formula. Remember to put it on the left side of your table, so you can use it with VLOOKUP.

Once you've created your helper column, you can write an ordinary lookup formula that uses it. For example, you can find a person in the list using the combined first and last name, like this:

=VLOOKUP(C1, A5:D32, 4, FALSE)

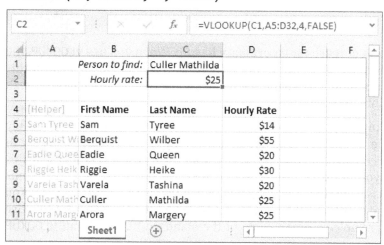

Pro tip: If you think the extra column looks too cluttered on your worksheet, you can make it vanish out of sight with Excel's hiding feature. Just right click the column header (in this example, that's the A heading at the top of the first column) and choose **Hide**. Excel still keeps your helper column and its data, but shrinks it down to be 0 pixels wide, so it's effectively invisible. (You can make a missing column reappear easily enough. Hover your mouse over the border where the column should be, until the mouse pointer turns into the double-arrow resize icon. Then, click and drag the missing column back into sight.)

How to get values on the left of your lookup

When you use VLOOKUP you find a value in a column, and then look for a piece of information on the right. But what if you want to look at a column on the left?

For example, look at this revised version of the customer table you saw earlier. Now there's a new column on the left, which records the date the customer was added.

This information is out of reach for an ordinary lookup. When you use VLOOKUP, the first column in your range needs to be the column with the lookup values (in this example, that's column B). But there is a way to break the rules. The trick is to break the lookup process into two steps.

The two classic lookup functions, VLOOKUP and HLOOKUP, do two things. First, they find the lookup value. Then, they fetch the information you want from elsewhere in the table. You've seen this two-step process unfold in plenty of examples in this chapter. But what you don't yet know is that you can perform these two steps *separately*. The trick is to use two more basic lookup functions: MATCH and INDEX. You use MATCH to find your lookup value. You then use INDEX to grab a nearby cell. Use them both, and you're able to break some of the standard VLOOKUP and HLOOKUP rules.

Let's try it out with the customer list. First you can use MATCH to perform the first step of a lookup—finding your lookup value:

```
=MATCH(D1, B5:B93)
```

When you call MATCH, you supply two parameters. First is the lookup value (in this case, that's the customer ID stored in cell D1). Second is the range of cells that represents your lookup column. The result of the MATCH function is a number that indicates the position of the match. For example, if the matching customer is in the third row, the MATCH function gives a result of 3. You can also call this number the *row index*.

The INDEX function does the second part of a lookup's job—it retrieves a value from another cell. INDEX needs two parameters. First is the cell range for the column with the data you want to retrieve. Second is the row index. For example, if you want to look at the date column and find the date the third customer was added, you could use a formula like this:

```
=INDEX(A5:A93, 3)
```

The real magic happens when you combine INDEX and MATCH by nesting the MATCH function inside INDEX. Here's how you perform your search with MATCH and then pass that row number to INDEX so it can get the data you want:

```
=INDEX(A5:A93, MATCH(D1, B5:B93))
```

	A	B	C	D
1			Type the Customer ID here:	ANTON
2			Date added:	7/6/2018
3				
4	Date Added	Customer ID	Company Name	Contact Name	Cont
5	10/23/2018	ALFKI	Alfreds Futterkiste	Maria Anders	Sales
6	7/6/2018	ANTON	Antonio Moreno Taqueria	Antonio Moreno	Owne
7	3/7/2018	AROUT	Around the Horn	Thomas Hardy	Sales
8	10/23/2018	BERGS	Berglunds snabbköp	Christina Berglund	Orde

And there you have it: a *left lookup*. It's a formula that matches a value in one column, and retrieves a corresponding value from a column on the left. The same technique works with HLOOKUP, except in this case the goal is to look at a row *above* your lookup row.

Using lookup lists

The last trick you'll learn in this chapter isn't just for lookups, but it works nicely with them. It's a feature called *lookup lists*, and it lets you save time (and avoid typos) by picking lookup values out of a list.

Think back to the customer list worksheet. Right now, you need to remember the customer ID and type it in yourself, without making a mistake. Imagine how much more convenient it would be if you could pick the customer you want from a handy list, like this:

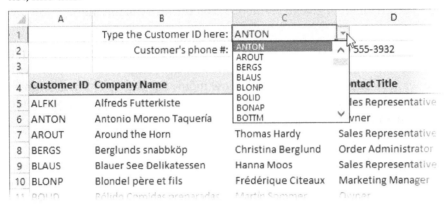

Creating a lookup list is easy. You simply need to tell Excel where in your spreadsheet it can find the list of acceptable values. Technically, the lookup list is part of Excel's *data validation* features, because it helps you prevent mistakes. The best way to understand how it works is to try it yourself.

Try it out: Make a lookup list

The following steps work with the Look Up! Catering spreadsheet from the tutorial earlier in this chapter. You'll add a lookup list that makes it easier to choose products when filling in an order.

1. Open the spreadsheet solution from the Look Up! Catering tutorial you did earlier in this chapter. You can download it using the link on the last step of the tutorial (at http://lab.halfwit2hero.com/excelformulas).

2. Select all the product ID cells (that's the column of cells from A5 to A30).

3. In the ribbon, choose **Data** ▷ **Data Tools** ▷ **Data Validation**. The Data Validation window will appear.

4. In the **Settings** tab, change the **Allow** setting to **List**.

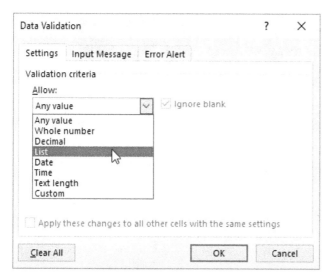

5. Click inside the **Source** box. This is where you'll fill in the list, by giving Excel a range of cells with the values you want to use.

6. In this example, the list needs to show all the product IDs. But don't bother typing the range in yourself. Instead, you can select it in the Excel window. Start by clicking the **Price List** worksheet tab. Then, click and drag to select the cells from A2 to A20.

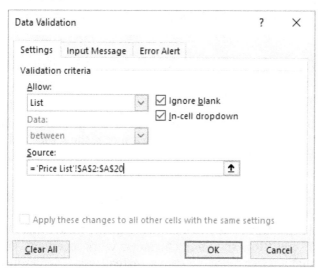

7. Click **OK** to add the list.

8. Now, whenever you're positioned on one of the product ID cells in column A, you'll see a down-pointing triangle appear next to the cell. Click it to show the list of product IDs.

Choose a product ID, and Excel inserts it into the cell. Not only is this truly convenient, it also makes sure you don't accidentally enter an ID for a product that doesn't exist.

The Last Word

Now that you're nearing the end of your Excel journey, it's a good time to stop and see how things have changed.

When you started out with Excel, you were writing simple formulas that worked mostly on their own. You might have used a cell reference here and there, but that was the most excitement you could expect.

As you've gained more experience with Excel, you've gone on to more complex examples. In the tutorial in this chapter, you worked with a spreadsheet that had two worksheets, each with its own table of data, and you wrote complex formulas to bring all these cells together and sidestep errors. Life clearly isn't the same.

This is also the point where Excel trainees start spending less time learning about functions and more time practicing the art of formula writing. For example, you'll start paying more attention to questions like "How do I arrange my data?" and "When do I use relative references?" and "How should my formulas work together?" Often, there are no absolute rules that answer these questions. Instead, you'll get a sense of what works best, most of the time, after you've had the chance to practice making some practical spreadsheets of your own.

Where to Go Next...

"At the end you arrive where you started, and know the place for the first time."

You've now spent ten chapters getting comfortable with Excel and the art of formula writing. You've tried out every major type of Excel function, from trigonometry to lookups. You've dealt with dates, times, text, and money. And you've learned many of the practical techniques that Excel heroes use to build formulas. So what happens next?

The Future of Excel and You

You may already know enough to close the book happy and get back to your real work. As you arrange more spreadsheets, write more formulas, and put the lessons from this book into practice, you'll become better and better at Excel formula writing.

You should also know enough to feel your way around someone else's fancy formula examples. That means when you face a new problem, you can take your search to the web, where you'll find plenty of tricks for specific scenarios. You may not know how to come up with these solutions on your own, but you *do* have the street smarts to take an online example and reconstruct it in your spreadsheet. (After all, that's what you've been doing all along for the exercises on the tutorial site.)

If you want to get even better at Excel formulas, there are plenty of advanced formula topics you can learn. People write entire books on obscure hacks that can stretch the limits of Excel. And as long as you aren't using the online version of Excel, you can use the Visual Basic programming language to write custom functions that can perform virtually any calculation you can imagine. (If you're curious, check out *Excel Programming for Dummies*, but don't let the name fool you—programming Excel is no small endeavor.)

If you're interested in expanding your Excel knowledge, your best option is to become familiar with other Excel features. If you haven't already studied charts, they're an essential ingredient for many spreadsheets, and the subject of the book *Excel Charts: Halfwit to Hero*. Charts are part of Excel's *data visualization* features—basically, the abilities Excel has to take your data and help you understand it. Excel has other data visualization features as well, including pivot tables (which let you break ginormous amounts of data down in tiny cross sections) and conditional formatting (which uses colors and icons to highlight important numbers). Excel masters can use these data visualization features to find hidden trends and relationships in huge piles of data. If any of these topics catch your interest, you can take to Google to learn more, or visit the Excel help center at http://support.office.com/excel.

You'll be happy to know that your formula-writing skills can stretch beyond Excel. Other programs, like Google Sheets, are designed to be as close to Excel as possible, with an identical system of cell references and many of the same functions.

Ultimately, it's up to you whether you decide to journey on with Excel or learn something new. If you'd like to share your feedback about this book, email matthew@prosetech.com. And stop by the Halfwit to Hero website (http://halfwit2hero.com) to see the current lineup of books and get news about future titles.

www.ingramcontent.com/pod-product-compliance
Lightning Source LLC
Chambersburg PA
CBHW060134060326
40690CB00018B/3872